D0348758

WITHDRAWN

1-800-DEADBEAT

HOW TO COLLECT
YOUR CHILD SUPPORT

SIMONE SPENCE

EGGSHELL PRESS
NEW YORK

Library of Congress Catalog Number: 99-90151
ISBN: 0-9670647-0-8
1. Child Support 2. Law and Legislation 3. United States 4. Popular works

First EggShell Press Edition: April 1999

10 9 8 7 6 5 4 3 2 1

Thank you to my husband, Alan, for his tireless efforts and for putting up with me while I finished this project. To my daughter, Storm, for being a wonderful helper and the best daughter that a Mom can have. To Dave, for his invaluable time and advice and to my legal team, many thanks.

"THE DUTY OF PARENTS TO PROVIDE FOR THE MAINTENANCE OF THEIR CHILDREN IS A PRINCIPAL OF NATURAL LAW... BY BEGETTING THEM, THEREFORE, THEY HAVE ENTERED INTO A VOLUNTARY OBLIGATION, TO ENDEAVOR, AS FAR AS IN THEM LIES, THAT THE LIFE WHICH THEY HAVE BESTOWED SHALL BE SUPPORTED AND PRESERVED. AND, THUS, THE CHILDREN WILL HAVE A PERFECT RIGHT OF RECEIVING MAINTENANCE FROM THEIR PARENTS.... AND IF A PARENT RUNS AWAY, AND LEAVES HIS CHILDREN, THE CHURCH WARDENS AND OVER-SEERS OF THE PARISH SHALL SEIZE HIS RANTS, GOODS, AND CHATTELS, AND, AND DISPOSE OF THEM TOWARDS THEIR RELIEF."

BLACKSTONE, 1750

WARNING

If your children are not receiving financial support from their non-custodial parent, then you, as their primary care giver, have the right to utilize any legal means necessary to get that parent to pay up. What you legally can not do, and should not do, in the best interest of your children, is to deny them the opportunity to have a relationship with the other parent. Understandably so, when a non-custodial parent refuses or has an inability to support their children, the parent who bares the responsibility solely may become frustrated, angry, and sometimes punitive towards the other responsible party. Use that anger to enforce your child support order, not to keep your children away from their other parent. If the non-custodial parent is abusive in any way or you feel that they are emotionally unhealthy, then take steps to protect your children during visitation. If your children do not have a relationship with the non-custodial parent let that parent make that decision. Please remember and try to separate love from money. Let your children love both of their parents, at the same time, insist that they be financially supported.

Table Of Contents

Table Of Items

Introduction

The history of child support orders and the enforcement of child support has been an outrage since the day "family law" first entered the legal system. Historically, the majority of custodial families have not had court ordered child support, and those receiving child support orders have rarely been awarded enough money to properly care for their children. Theoretically, child support awards should to be sufficient enough to mimic the same economic advantages a child would have if his or her parents were together as a couple. Once the court has ordered child support, most custodial parents still have a hard time collecting any child support monies. Some families are able to get partial payments, while some families get no payments at all.

Fortunately not all custodial families experience the economic abuse of child support evasion. The sad truth is, however, that only 25% of families that have child support awards ever collect. This book is not gender specific. It is not written to tag men or non-custodial fathers as deadbeats, although some of them are. It is written for any custodial parent, male or female that needs help to get financial support for their children. 87% of custodial parents are women. The remaining 13% are men, grandparents, and others. There are deadbeat dads, and there are deadbeat moms. In some instances both dad and mom are deadbeats. It does not matter what gender the deadbeat parent is. The object of this ball game is to get them to financially support their children.

Some of the techniques in this book, when used properly, may cause embarrassment to the deadbeat. Some techniques can cause a business person to lose his or her credibility and can cause financial ruin for some. That is the point. A custodial parent should feel little sympathy for someone that they have had to drag into court to get them to financially support their child. Many custodial parents are ashamed that they have to force their child's other parent to pay. After all, supporting their own flesh and blood should be something that they want to do. Others do not want to cause the other parent to become angry. It's a common misconception that a non-custodial parent will be more likely to pay child support if they are not forced and if the amount of child support is low. In the eighteenth century, judges would award nominal child support awards in the belief that there would be little animosity towards a lower amount. That process of thought only causes more difficulties. Children suffer due to a lack of economic stability and often even the lower amount of money is not paid. That tactic did not work 200 years ago and it does not work now. To award a low amount of support trivializes its' need and meaning. Sometimes custodial parents feel that they want to raise their child on their own, without any help from the other parent. Mostly they just want the problem to go away. Be assured that by getting child support you are doing the right thing for your child. Children deserve support from both parents and the problem will not go away on it's own.

Part of the problem with custodial families enforcing their child support orders has been the non-support of our government. Bureaucrats can talk themselves blue in the face over solving this issue of parental responsibility, but it has been around for centuries and not enough has been done to change it. We as a nation have not decided whether child support is a legal issue or a moral issue. Should financial responsibility of our children be something that is morally the right thing to do, or is it a matter that we should enforce legally like other civil monetary disputes and to what degree?

There lays the rub. Some believe that it is more of a morality or "family" issue to support one's children and some believe that it is nothing more than a legal or "state" issue. It can be argued that it is a choice between "free exercise of families," meaning that families have the choice of how they want to interact with each other, versus "public moral ordering", meaning that the government can decide what is best for families. Should each family decide for themselves if, when, how, and how much child support should be paid, or should the government ensure that it will be done? You can see how it becomes a dilemma. The question then becomes which came first, the chicken or the egg. Whose moral codes do we use when deciding child support? As long as child support is considered a domestic or a family issue, we as a nation will always be split on how it is viewed.

As mentioned before, the obligation to support one's children has been around since the seventeenth century and developed in the nineteenth century under family law. Up until the nineteenth century, fathers were awarded custody of their children. This is largely due to the fact that, since women did not work outside of the home, they were unable to financially support them. In the late eighteenth century women began to get custody if they had some visible means of support and if the father was at fault in the divorce. At this time, industrialization and the growth of factories moved production out of the households and off the farms so as to require less help of the children of the household. Women also at this time began to take paid-labor positions, despite public disapproval.

Soon thereafter, for reasons still under debate by historical scholars, the Social Security Act of 1935 was created and included both Old Age Insurance (Social Security as we know it) and Aid to Dependent Children. Aid to Dependent Children (ADC) was created to replace a mother's pension or mother's aid program that had been created to provide assistance to "deserving" (mostly widows) single mothers and their children. In 1962 ADC was renamed AFDC (Aid to Families with Dependent Children). The AFDC dole remained low until the mid - 1960's. From 1965-1973 AFDC nearly doubled its participants and expenditures due to the rise of divorce, out of wedlock births, and the rise of the civil rights and welfare movements. All of a sudden the government began to notice a problem.

In 1974, the federal government established Title IV-D of the Social Security Act to set up federally mandated, state-implemented agencies to aid custodial parents in obtaining child support awards and collect from non-custodial parents. The government's main priority in establishing Title IV-D was to the custodial parents that were on AFDC, not to custodial families on the whole; although non-AFDC families were allowed the same services. The program was developed to collect child support from non-custodial parents so as to lessen the financial load on the federal government. When written it was "directed at the goal of achieving or maintaining economic self-support to prevent, reduce, or eliminate dependency." Other amendments of the Social Security Act are the Child Support Enforcement Amendments of 1984 (CSEA), and the Family Support Act of 1988 (FSA); both were aimed at strengthening child support enforcement practices through paternity establishment and the collection and disbursement of child support payments. Among other things, the FSA also required that states establish and implement mandatory child support guidelines to produce some level of continuity with child support awards.

Seemingly, child support enforcement has had Congressional support. However, the federal child support program no longer provides overall cost savings. That was its original goal, to provide cost savings to federal government by forcing parental responsibility. The federal government supports the costs of the program, while states receive income from it. In fiscal year 1993, child support collections totaled $8.9 billion while administrative costs of the program exceeded AFDC collection by $278 million, or 3.1 percent of total collections.

Because the original goal of cost savings is no longer being realized, 23 million children are owed an excess of $34 billion dollars in overdue child support.

The time has come to take matters into your own hands. You cannot wait for a system that is in need of repair to collect your child support. Caseworkers are overloaded. While you can still use the services the government has to offer you, you must also be your own advocate. Remember your caseworker is there to earn a paycheck; you need to put food on your table and clothes on your child's back. It does not matter where you are in life right now. You can be an AFDC recipient, or a wealthy business owner; your child still needs and deserves financial support. If you do not need the money to raise your child, then put the funds into a college account.

Many custodial parents use their divorce attorney to handle their child support case. If you can afford one that's good for you, but do not count solely on their expertise to get your money. Family law is not an extremely lucrative field, especially when it comes to the collection of child support. Most garden-variety family law attorneys are not aware of most of the tools this book will introduce to you. If you are going to use an attorney, read this book from front to back and the next time you have a conversation with her or him, ask about a few of the things you have learned. You may be surprised to find that you now know as much as, or frightfully more, than your attorney. The knowledge you will have once you have completed this book will take you far in your pursuit of child support.

Chapter 1: Establishing Your Child Support Order

When Marsha and her son's father "Doug", separated, they agreed that he would pay child support to her directly instead of going through the "child support system." In her mind, it would be less of a hassle because she would always know when she was getting her money, and she thought that it would cause less ruffled feathers. She didn't want "Doug" to get angry with her and decide not to pay anything at all. It was also less of a hassle for her. Who wanted to go to the child support agency and wait around all day anyway? She had visions of an unemployment office or a welfare office in her mind, and she did not want any part of it. She somehow felt that she was doing something wrong if she had to ask for help to get child support for her daughter.

Her ex made regular child support payments for about six months before the money abruptly stopped. For six months he promised that the money would come, but, of course, it never did. Marsha did not know what to do and no one that she asked knew either. She never thought that her ex would do anything like that. She trusted his word that he would pay child support as he promised and she almost lost everything that she had because of it.

The moral of the story is, if you have a child and are not in a committed relationship where both parents live with the child and equally support the child, then you should get a *child support award* from the court. *Volunteer agreements* usually do not work. Typically, the *non-custodial* parent will pay them on a regular basis and then for whatever reason, the payments either stop or they do not come regularly anymore. Usually, the *non-custodial* parent has found himself or herself in another relationship and is spending more money to maintain that relationship. There can be a variety of reasons: new car purchase, vacation, new home, wardrobe, etc. Some *non-custodial* parents have been known to hold back child support when they are angry with the *custodial* parent. They use the child's support money as a means of punishment and reward and control; whatever the reason, it is wrong and you and your child do not need to be a part of it. For this reason, this book recommends that you immediately get a child support award from the court following the break-up of a love relationship, or when a child is born out-of-wedlock.

You can insist that child support be *court-ordered* without being angry about it. You should always be as calm, cool, and collected as you can. It may be very difficult at times, especially when you want to shout your head off or wring somebody's neck. You will always get more honey away from the bee if you do not kick the beehive. A conversation with your child's other parent might go something like this:

> You: Charlie, since we have decided to separate, I think that we should have a formal court ordered child support agreement. That way, we can both keep accurate records of payments and we will both know that whatever arrangements that we have is fair. It will be less likely that we will have disagreements between us. Let's sit down and go over the expenses for (your child's name). Let's try to come to a fair agreement between us. If we

cannot, then we can go before a judge and have it decided for us.

Your ex:	You don't trust me?
You:	It's not that I don't trust you, I just think that it will be easier this way. We both have a lot of healing to do from this break-up and I think that it will be one less thing for us to worry about.

~or~

You:	Brian, I am so happy that we have a child together. Even though we are not married, I know that you love (your child's name) and me. There is something that I would like for us to do. Futures can be so uncertain, so for your protection and mine, and most importantly for (your child's name), I want to have a fair agreement between us for financial support so that we will not have any misunderstandings.
Your ex:	What is this about, don't you trust me?
You:	Of course I trust you! This is not about trust. I just want to make sure that we have as little to argue about as possible. As new parents we will not agree on everything, and I am sure that there will be times that we are stressed out; we do not need to argue about something as silly as money. I would rather not ask you for money when the baby needs something. If I have regular support coming in, I will be able to budget accordingly.

    You will notice that in the first example the *custodial* parent suggested that the two parents come to some type of monetary agreement together and submit it to the court, and

3

previously I suggested that *volunteer agreements* are not a good idea. I am not contradicting myself. By the end of this chapter you will have a better idea of what your expenses are as a result of being a *custodial* parent. If you are offered an amount that is not fair and you are not able to re-negotiate it with the *non-custodial* parent, you can then decide what is in your best interest; whether you should accept it or go to court. In any case, it is my opinion that you should always get court ordered payments unless you are dealing with a God-like creature that worships his or her children and the ground they walk on. In that case, the only precaution would be to keep an amount equal to a few months' child support in the bank so that if "Mr. Creature of God- Like Perfection" turns out to be your worst nightmare, you can make it through the months it would take to track him down and get money from him. That's right, *months.*

Not trusting your financial future to someone that may or may not pay your child's support on time is only one reason to go through the court system. The other is to make sure that you are getting a fair deal. Your ex may offer to give you forty dollars a week to support his or her child. At first, you may think that it is a good offer. This book will help you to take a closer look to determine what your child's needs are and what amount is necessary for upkeep. Usually people forget the little things that add up to great sums of money in the end. Things like weekly allowances, school lunches, and school trips are often forgotten when calculating support monies. Then there are things that sometimes are not considered in the first place, but they should be. An example might be extra medical expenses that are not covered by an insurance plan. The following list will help you to determine what you spend, or will be spending, on an average month to care for your child. Go through the list on the following pages and fill in the blanks as they apply to you.

CHILD RELATED EXPENSES CHECKLIST

Rent/Mortgage   _____
House/Apt. Insurance   _____
Taxes   _____
Water/Sewer   _____
Repairs   _____
Gas/Electric   _____
Phone   _____
Garbage   _____
Food   _____
Household Supplies   _____
Clothes   _____
Laundry/Dry Cleaning   _____
Clothing Repair   _____
Car Payment   _____
Car Insurance   _____
Car Repair   _____
Public Transportation _____
Child Care   _____
Babysitters   _____
Medical Insurance   _____
Medical Needs Not Covered _____
Dental Visits   _____
Vision Visits   _____
Prescriptions   _____
School Payments   _____
School Supplies   _____
School Trips   _____
School Lunches   _____
Dance, Music Lessons, etc. _____
Extracurricular Activities _____
Barber/Beauty Shop   _____
Religious Affiliation _____

Sub-Total - This page _____

CHILD RELATED EXPENSES CHECKLIST

Religious Schooling   _____
Books/Magazines   _____
Pets   _____
Vacation   _____
Gifts To Others   _____
Allowance   _____

Sub-Total   _____
Sub-Total - Previous Page _____

Total Expenses   _____

Now that you have a better idea of what expenses you incur as you raise your child, you may not want to jump at the first offer of financial support you get. At the same time, it does not give you the right to pad your expenses to try to get more money either. Besides, knowing your expenses is only a starting ground. You have to know what to do when you get the information.

The first thing you must do when you are ready to file for child support is to decide whether you want to handle your case yourself or if you want the state to work your case for you. Whether you handle it yourself or get the state agency to do it for you, all of the procedures remain the same. The only difference is that you retain complete control of your case if you do it yourself, but you will also have more legwork to do on your own. If the state handles your case you end up at their mercy while they work the case on your behalf. Since they are the ones that will be filing motions with the court system, you will largely remain in the dark and will have to push them to advise you of any progress made. You can at any time decide to change paths if you choose a method that does not seem to work for you. If you have decided to let the state agency collect your support, you can take the case back from them at any time (providing that you are not on welfare), and vice versa. The methods that you use to enforce your child support order will remain the same regardless of who collects the money. Which method should you choose? It's a personal choice and only you can make that decision. If you want complete control of your case and don't mind some of the headaches, collect your support on your own. If you don't mind losing some control and would rather if someone else did most of the legwork for you, then let the agency work on your behalf. To keep matters simple since most people opt to have the state child support agencies collect their support for them, we will assume that everyone wants to. Keep in mind that it is your choice and you can change your mind at any time. If you are working with an attorney, you can still receive benefits from the state agency. Likewise, if you are handling your case on your own you can receive benefits from the agencies and vice-versa. Many *custodial parents* are routinely told that they cannot have it both ways, but that is not true. Be sure to speak with someone who knows; your caseworker may not.

The first thing that you must do when you are ready to file for child support is to locate the nearest *child support agency (if you filing on your own locate the Family Court in your area).* Every state has several child support enforcement agencies that are obligated, by law, to help you obtain a child support award and enforce your child support order once you get one. You can begin by calling your local welfare office and asking them to direct you to the closest child support agency. Although child support agencies and welfare agencies are not related, they sometimes work together. Many custodial parents end up on welfare because the non-custodial parent does not pay child support.

When you call the agency you can ask them to mail an application to you. There is a Federal law that states that, as of October 1993, applications must be provided within 5 days if they are mailed, or upon request if you visit the office. If time allows, pick up the application. The application should be self-explanatory. If it is not, do not hesitate to make an appointment to have someone help you complete it. You will be asked to bring in certain documentation when you go to the agency for your intake. This book recommends that you get a folder, large envelope, or shoebox of some sort so that you can begin to collect the data that will help you. Although it may vary, generally this is the information that you will need to bring on your first visit:

INTAKE DOCUMENTATION

1. Birth Certificates for the child
2. Your Identification
3. Your Social Security Number
4. Child's Social Security Number
5. Other Parent's Social Security Number
6. Last Known Address of Other Parent
7. Last Known Employer of Other Parent
8. As many current photos that you can find of the absent parent.

If your local agency does not ask for all of this information, do your best to bring it in anyway. The more information you have about the absent parent, the better. The agency will need to contact the absent parent's employer to determine how much he or she makes. It will make life much easier for everyone involved, especially you, if they already know who the employer is. If paternity has not been established at the time of your visit to the agency, you will also want to bring:

1. Records of any money the absent parent has given to you for the child
2. Records of any gifts that the absent parent has given the child

After all the information that you can supply has been provided, the absent parent will be served with papers requiring him or her to submit information on his or her income, occupation, current address, etc. A court date will then be arranged. Usually, a hearing officer rather than a judge hears child support cases, but it could be either. You and the absent parent will be notified of when you must appear in court, and when you do, an order of support will be entered. Child support that is awarded will be retroactive to the date that you filed your motion in the child support agency; sometimes that could be a month or two. What that means is that the absent parent will owe you for several months already! For example, let us presume that you filed a motion for child support on July 1, and you finally got your day in court on August 15.   If the hearing officer awarded you $75 a week in child support, the absent parent would now owe you 6 weeks of child support, or $450! So if you are going to file for financial support for your child, the sooner you do it, the better.

Before 1989, judges had considerable discretion when formulating child support awards. Because of that, wealthy absent parents sometimes paid very little, and poor absent parents sometimes were ordered to pay more than their monthly income. The biggest tragedy, however, was that in most instances child support awards were inadequate to meet the true cost of raising children.   Thankfully, in 1988, federal *legislation* was passed (Family Support Act), which ordered all states to establish a guideline for determining child support. This helps child support awards to be more fair and realistic. Every state was ordered to adopt one of three child support formulas.

INCOME SHARES

The income shares formula considers the income of both parents and assumes that they will equally share the costs of raising their child together. It tries to base the support on the concept that the child should receive the same level of financial support that he or she would have received if the parents lived together. The income of both parents is combined. A chart listing the support amount for that level of income is checked. The support amount is then prorated between each parent according to his or her income. Thirty-three states, Guam, and the Virgin Islands use this formula. The following is a complete list of states that have adopted the Income Shares Model.

Alabama	New Jersey
Arizona	New Hampshire
California	New York
Colorado	North Carolina
Connecticut	Ohio
Florida	Oklahoma
Idaho	Oregon
Indiana	Pennsylvania
Iowa	Rhode Island
Kansas	South Carolina
Kentucky	South Dakota
Louisiana	Utah
Maryland	Vermont
Maine	Virginia
Michigan	Washington
Missouri	West Virginia
Nebraska	

Oregon is a state that uses the income shares formula; an example based on the income shares is listed below:

Custodial parent's monthly earnings	$823.00
Non-custodial parent's monthly earnings	$2,650.00
Combined earnings total	$3473.00
Percentage of custodial parent's share	13.7%
Percentage of non-custodial parent's share	76.3%
Child support obligation	$488.00
Childcare costs	$170.00
Total child support obligation	$658.00
Custodial parent's child support obligation	$155.95
Non-custodial parent's child support obligation	$ 502.05

PERCENT OF INCOME FORMULA

The percent of income formula uses only the *non-custodial* parent's income to determine a child support award. It is the easiest method to use since all that is done is a simple mathematical deduction. For example, Wisconsin deducts seventeen (17) percent of a non-custodial parent's gross income for support of one child. That figure increases slightly for each additional child. In Delaware, however, the percentage is eighteen (18) percent and it is deducted from the non-custodial parent's net income, and as in Wisconsin, the percentage increases slightly with each child. (Gross income is the amount of salary that a person receives before taxes are taken out, and net income is the amount that a person is left with after taxes are deducted).

The states that use the percentage of income formula are:

Alaska	Mississippi
Arkansas	Nevada
District Of Columbia	North Dakota
(Washington D. C.)	Puerto Rico
Georgia	Texas
Illinois	Wisconsin
Minnesota	Wyoming

MELSON FORMULA

Only three states have chosen to adopt the Melson Formula. Unlike the other two-guideline types, the Melson formula sets aside a "self-support reserve" for each parent before determining their ability to pay. What it does is allows each parent to subtract the dollar amount from their salary that is needed to keep them at poverty level before child support payments are considered. Once each parent's reserve amount is calculated and subtracted from their salary, child support can then be determined. The three states that use the Melson Formula are:

Delaware   Montana
Hawaii

The guidelines generally work well for most people *if* the amount is determined based on everything your child needs. Frequently parents forget what they spend on their children. Use the "child related expenses" list located at the beginning of this chapter. If you get a child support order that you feel is too low, or have forgotten too many items, or were never told to include certain items in the first place (which happens very often), you can get your child support order modified. Chapter 4 deals with *modifying* child support orders.

In the meantime, other items should be included in your child support order other than child support itself. Medical insurance should be a part of your child support order. The absent parent should be required to include the child on his or her plan at work. If no plan is available, you can and should ask for more child support to cover the costs of a private policy.

Life insurance should also be a part of your child support award. If the non-custodial parent should die unexpectedly, your child support payments will stop. If you do not have life insurance as a part of your child support award already, you should ask for more child support to cover the costs of a life insurance policy. Naturally, your child will be listed as the beneficiary.

Child support awards are not final. They can and should be reviewed every three years. All three guideline formulas recognize that children become more expensive as they grow older, so the three year review period allows for the custodial parent to request an increase. If you cannot wait because your support award does not include medical or life insurance, you can file a motion for a modification. An explanation of how to file a modification motion is outlined in chapter four.

Chapter 2: Establishing Paternity

If you were not married to your child's father at the time of his or her birth, you will need to *establish paternity* in order to receive court ordered child support. This means that you will have to prove who the father of the baby is. When children are born between two people who are married, the law assumes that the husband of the woman who gave birth is the father of the child. When the woman is not married, she must prove who fathered her child in order to get the court system to order child support. Child support payments can always be paid voluntarily by the father, but as discussed in Chapter 1, "Obtaining your court order", it is not recommended in most cases.

I know a father that pays child support to his ex girlfriend on a voluntary agreement that they have together. According to him, they do not need a formal order. Whatever their daughter needs, their daughter gets. While that sounds very "knight in shining armourish," I wonder if they are really splitting their child's expenses fairly. The mother has custody of the child and lives in another state. Even with court ordered child support awards, the custodial parent usually ends up taking on more than 50% of the load. On the other hand, I know many fathers that bend over backward to do much more than their fair share. It's a character judgment, and only you can make the call.

The easiest way to establish paternity is during what I call "happy hour." That is when the child is first born and lying in the nursery, cute with rosy cheeks. The entire family has gathered around and friends have come from near and far to see the new baby. Of course, proud Papa is standing by grinning ear to ear at his newest creation, almost intoxicated by the miracle of it all. This is the time that most fathers would proudly announce their fatherhood.

Have him sign the birth certificate then and there. By putting his name on the certificate of birth he is admitting that he has fathered the child. In most states, that will be all you need in a court of law.

If he does not want to sign the birth certificate, or "happy hour" is long gone and you do not have an admission of paternity, you already know that you are going to have a problem. Get him to write a *letter of consent* stating that he is the father of your child. Use your discretion. You can tell him why you want this letter if you do not think that he will go home and immediately begin to pack his bags. You can also make up some hokey sentimental story about the two of you writing letters to your newborn child, whatever works.

Now, let's say that the man you believe to be the baby's father refuses to sign his name on the birth certificate or write a letter of consent. You can then have a *paternity* test ordered. A *paternity* test is a test that can be given to a suspected father to either prove or disprove that he has fathered a child. There are many different types of tests that can be administered. They involve testing you, your child and the suspected father, so you must wait until the baby is born before you begin.

The most common type of paternity test today, in most states, is the *Buccal Swab Sampling*. In this procedure a long Q-tip type stick is rubbed along the inside of the mouth of you, the suspected father, and your child to collect cells that determine

14

DNA. The swab is sent to a lab for the *DNA* of the suspected father to be compared with that of the child in question. This test along with other genetic procedures that can be performed can determine fatherhood with 99.99% accuracy. Other common tests include the blood test when blood is drawn from both parties, and umbilical cord sampling where part of the umbilical cord of a newborn is sent in for testing.

These tests are familiar to most people. What the majority of people do not know, is that paternity can be proven even if the suspected father is deceased or has been lost in the Alps Mountains for years, without a trace.

Let's say that you become pregnant and you and your boyfriend are planning to be married even though his family has expressed their strong dislike for you. Before your wedding day, a terrible accident occurs and your boyfriend is killed. You were not married to him so the law can not assume that he fathered your baby. His family doubts your boyfriend's paternity and will not help with your expenses. Meanwhile, bills are piling up and you do not have anyone to help you. To top it all off, your boyfriend was rich beyond belief. What do you do? Simple; you either have a *family calculation study* ordered (which tests the suspected father's family members for matching *DNA*), or you have *forensic paternity testing* or *abnormal specimen testing* performed. These are tests that can be done at the medical examiner's office before your boyfriend is buried, or after he has been buried you can order that his body be exhumed (removed from the ground), and tested for *DNA* matches. Sounds gruesome, I know.

Desperate times call for desperate measures. If it will keep your child out of poverty, it is well worth it.

Now let us imagine that your boyfriend is not dead, but instead says that he will die before he admits to you or anyone else that he is the father of your baby. In fact, he says he will refuse to take a paternity test so that you can not prove his fatherhood. Do not let this type of threat keep you from establishing paternity for your child. He is trying to make you believe that if he does not take a test, you can not prove his fatherhood. Maybe he really believes that himself. The fact of

15

the matter is that you have the law on your side. If you file a paternity suit against the suspected father, by law, he has no choice but to show up for the *DNA* testing. If he does not show, he automatically loses, and you win. It's called *default*. You have not confirmed that he is the father, but you have won your case by default, because he did not show up to defend himself, and to prove that he is not the father. You can then begin your pursuit for court ordered child support. The only way the father can get out of having a judgement for child support entered against him is if he takes the test and the *DNA* does not match. This will be the only thing that will prove that he is not the baby's father. So if the suspected father threatens to refuse testing, do not let it bother you one bit. Just smile and fill out the paperwork as quickly as you can.

Now let us imagine that you do not know who the father is. You were dating two men at the same time. You slept with guy # 1 for the last time three weeks before you slept with guy #2. A month later you are pregnant, and can not be absolutely sure who the father is. In this case, both men can be suspected fathers and you will have to have both of them tested. Remember, however, that if you have only slept with these two men, one of them will be excluded completely as being the father of the baby, and the other will be proven to be the father undoubtedly.

If you lose your paternity case it could mean only one of two things. There is another man that needs to be tested, or that the lab somehow went awry. You can ask to have the test repeated, but the labs rarely, if ever, make mistakes.

If you have an attorney, she or he will prepare the necessary paperwork to get the tests ordered so that paternity can be established for your child. If you do not have an attorney, you must contact your local child support enforcement agency. See appendix A for a listing of these central offices. Call the number listed and ask them where the closest agency is to your home. Your local agency will ask you to fill out paperwork regarding the relationship between you and the suspected father, any other intimate relationships you may have had at the same time, and your pregnancy. You may also be asked to provide certain documentation; such as a birth certificate for your child, medical records, etc. A caseworker will then contact the suspected father and ask him to consent to paternity. If he does, paternity has been established and a court date for child support will be arranged. If he does not consent, then *genetic* testing will be ordered. Depending on your income, you may have to help pay for the tests ordered. If you are *indigent*, you will not be asked to pay for the tests.

At this point you may be asking yourself why anyone would bother to go through all of this. That's a good question, and there are some very good answers.

Once paternity has been established, children born out of wedlock have equal benefits as those who were born within a marriage. This means that they can not be discriminated against for any reason. If one child is entitled to two peas, then the other child is entitled to two peas. Children who are born between two people who are married, or who have had their paternity proven if his or her parents were not married, are entitled to many things. They are entitled to child support payments if the parents separate, medical and life insurance, social security benefits, veteran's benefits, if any, and rights to inheritance. You will want to establish paternity even if your boyfriend does not have a job. Just because he does not have one today, does not mean he will not have one for the rest of his life.   Chapter 9 will explain how you can get child support from someone that does not have a job.

There are some women that choose not to establish paternity for their child. They are well aware of the benefits that their child will receive, but to them the drawbacks are more serious. By proving paternity in court, you are forcing a father to assume responsibility of fatherhood; financial responsibility; at least. The other side of the token is that the father now has a parental right to that child. So they may then, if they already have not, file an action for visitation. Some mothers fear this because they do not want the father in the child's life for some reason. Maybe they feel that the father is mentally unstable or abusive.

Without legal paternity, a suspected father can not exercise any rights to see his child.

This is a rather personal decision, and the law allows paternity to be established up to the child's eighteen birthday. Keep in mind however, that the child will not be entitled to child support or other benefits, and you will be on your own financially. Also keep in mind that the suspected father can take you to court at any time for paternity and visitation. You might as well beat him to the punch and allow your child the financial rewards of having two parents that contribute to her or his well being. If you are truly concerned about the safety of your child, you can ask for supervised visitation. Be sure to have a good reason for asking for it in the first place.

Some suspected fathers will use visitation as a threat to the mother of the child. They may threaten that if the mother takes them to court for paternity, that they will take them to court for visitation of the child. Sometimes this is enough to cause a mother to reconsider her options. Keep in mind however, that a father has a right to see his child, so he may end up taking you to court at any time. Do you really want to live with this hanging over your head? Besides, any father, or suspected father in this case, that would make that kind of threat really has no interest in his child anyway. So threats of visitation, or actual visitation, would probably go away as quickly as they came.

If the suspected father is incarcerated, is in another state or has left the country, chapters 8, 14, and 18 on finding your deadbeat, Interstate Collection and International Collection will give you information on how to find out where they are so that you can continue your paternity case. The same rules that apply for locating deadbeats that have skipped out on their children will apply for locating suspected fathers.

Chapter 3: Teens And Grand Parents As Parents

STATISTICS:
1. One out of every four children born in the United States today is born out of wedlock.
2. Only 25% of custodial parents who were not married at the time of their child(ren)'s birth obtain a child support order.
3. 75% of custodial parents that were married to the non-custodial parent at the time of their child(ren)'s birth do obtain child support orders.

The majority of children that are born outside of wedlock are born to teen-age parents. Many others are born to couples who are living together, but not married. When teens become parents they are confronted with special issues that others do not have.

In most instances underage parents are not married. As discussed in chapter two, "Establishing Paternity," the law assumes that the husband of the woman who gave birth is the father of her child. If she is not married, as far as the law is concerned, the baby does not have a father. Paternity will have to be established before she is able to claim who the father of her child is and get child support from the baby's father. Most pregnant teen moms live in the hallucination that they will be together with their child's father forever. This prevents them from seeking court ordered support on the basis that it might harm their relationship. Their musings are not a figment of their imagination. Often, the father pledges "forever" to relieve himself of any immediate responsibility of fatherhood. Here and now is replaced by promises of a wonderful future together. So instead of filing a paternity action after the birth of their child, most teenage mothers go through the process and discovery of how much it costs to raise a baby on their own. A small percentage will eventually take the father to court once it becomes evident that promises for support will not be kept. The rest carry the load on their own.

The difference between a teen unmarried mother and an adult unmarried mother is that for the most part, the adult mother has had the opportunity to finish school and maybe get a decent job to support herself. That alone does not mean that the custodial parent in this case will survive financially. Without child support, many women end up on AFDC (Aid to Families with Dependent Children). 87% of the women on welfare are there because they do not get child support. An education will at least, hopefully, give the woman some type of head start. Most teen-age parents do not have this benefit.

If you are a teen-age parent, the information that is outlined in this book for paternity actions and child support enforcement apply to you as well. You should pursue your child support case in the same manner. Many teen parents feel that it is useless to petition for child support since chances are that the father of the child does not have a job, or he has one that pays very little. That may be true. At some point however, he will become employed or his income will increase. It may be in the distant future so it will not help you or your baby now. When he finally does become employed, if you have successfully received your order for support, he will owe you money that will be in the *arrears*. *Arrears* are money that is owed to you, but that has not been paid.

FOR EXAMPLE:
Let's say that your child's father is 16 years old. He lives with his parents and they support him completely. He does not have a job. Your child is born and the father cannot contribute anything financially. You have one of two options:

Option # 1: You decide that it does not make sense to take him to court for money because he does not have any to give to you. Besides, you know that you cannot get any child support unless you establish paternity first and that involves testing. You have been through enough already with the pregnancy and the birth of your child and you do not want to be bothered. You decide to wait until he finishes high school and gets a real job making some real money. He has promised to take care of you and your baby then. Two years later, your boyfriend graduates from high school and gets a job, but he still does not give you any money to help support your child. After a considerable amount of thought you finally decide to take the difficult steps of filing a paternity action to establish parentage and to get child support. Months later, after you have had your day in court, your boyfriend has been ordered to pay $60 a week, and you have just received your first $60 check. You will get $60 a week, every week. That's $240 a month.

Option # 2: You take your boyfriend to court immediately for paternity and financial support of your child. Months later, after you have had your day in court, your boyfriend has been ordered to pay $60 a week. You do not get any money now because your boyfriend does not have an income. Two years later, your boyfriend graduates from high school and gets a job. You inform your case worker of where your boyfriend is working. A few weeks later you receive your first check of $340. You will get $340 a month, one hundred dollars more than your child support order states he must pay until he pays off the past due child support.

The day you file for child support is the day that your

child's father begins to owe. If it is found that he is not the father, then of course, he will owe nothing. If he is the father, then the debt continues to accumulate. When he begins to make payments, he will then owe his regular child support amount, plus an additional amount to pay for the two years that he did not pay anything.

It's the same two years without getting any money, while your boyfriend finishes school, but the outcomes are completely different. You decide which choice makes more sense for you.

When you are underage you are a minor by law. In most states your parent or guardian will have to petition the court as guardian "ad litem" for child support for your child. This means that they are standing up for you in court since you have no voice according to the law. Your boyfriend's parent or guardian may have to stand up for him as well. It's part of the price you pay when you have a baby before you are eighteen.

It's an interesting fact that most underage girls do not become pregnant by underage boys at all, but by adult males in their twenties, and sometimes older. An older father changes things substantially, so act accordingly.

****

An increasing number of grandparents have been stepping up to the plate to raise their grandchildren. Typically, these children are abandoned by their parents, are on drugs, incarcerated, or are otherwise unable to care for them. If this is your case, you will not be able to get child support unless you have some type of legal guardianship over the child. Simply taking the child off their parents hands for a while is not enough. If you want child support, you must go through the child support system.

You can get child support from both parents if the child is in your care. Once you get guardianship, your child support documents will be filed against both parents, instead of just one. You will follow the same procedures as everyone else, with the only difference being: you get double the trouble! Contact your local child support office to get started.

Chapter 4: Modification Of Your Child Support Order

There may be a time when the amount of child support you receive does not seem as if it's enough. You may be taking money out of your pocket to cover costs that are not basic living necessities and therefore were not accounted for when you applied for child support. Items like birthday party gifts, school functions, school supplies and trips are often forgotten when calculating child support.

If you have already been awarded child support by going to court but do not believe that the amount ordered is fair and sufficient enough to raise your child, you can *appeal* the court's decision. When I refer to "the court" I am referring to the person at the court that made the decision about your child support. The phrase "the court" is frequently used by attorneys and other court personnel so it's a good idea for you to become used to hearing it and reading about it. Throughout this chapter I will either use the terms "the court" or the decision - maker. They are the ones that decide what happens with your child support. It is up to them to decide who owes, who pays and how much. Decision-makers can differ from state to state. You can end up with any of the three choices. An appeal means that you do not agree with the decision made by the court and that you want your case heard again so that another decision can possibly be made. Appeals can be tricky. You should only file for an appeal if you are certain that the amount of child support that has been ordered falls below the child support guidelines for your state or if there is a considerable amount of information that would benefit you that was not considered when the original decision was made. This is true whether you are appealing your case or if your child support award was okay when you first received it but it's been awhile and you feel that it's time for your award to be increased. Either way you should be careful when you are preparing your case because of the rule of *estoppel*. The rule of estoppel says that you can not bring something up at a later time in order to change a decision if you knew about the information beforehand, but did not reveal it.

FOR EXAMPLE:

A divorced couple agrees to an amount of child support. This agreed upon amount is written into their divorce decree, and it is now permanent. The ex-husband later decides that he is paying too much and files papers to have the child support lowered. His reasoning is that his ex-wife's second job income was not considered when they calculated income and expenses to arrive at a child support amount comfortable for the two of them. This is where the law of *estoppel* is used. Since the husband knew about the second job income when the decision for child support was made, he was not able to get his child support payment lowered.

Although I said that the couple's child support award was made permanent in their divorce decree, nothing is ever permanent in the child support world; it's only temporarily permanent. Permanent, that is, until something changes to make the current child support award not fair or sufficient anymore, and until someone makes a move to do something about it. The Federal Child Support Act of 1988 says that your local child support enforcement agency will review your child support case every three years. If a sufficient amount of financial considerations have changed, your case will be reviewed and the child support amount may be increased. But, as they say, — don't hold your breath. The child support agencies are so back logged its difficult enough for them to handle a regular caseload. So in order to keep up with your child support case it's up to you to determine whether there has been a *change in circumstances* significant enough to warrant going to court.

A *change in circumstances* occurs when financial matters have changed considerably rendering the original child support order unfair or insufficient. A change might result in one of two decisions; an *upward modification* of the child support order, or a *downward modification* of the child support order. An *upward modification* is an increase in child support and a *downward modification* is a decrease.

CHANGE OF CIRCUMSTANCES:

The absent parent gets a new job, or increases his/her income through a higher salary or bonus.

The standards for how much of an increase in salary is sufficient to grant an *upward modification* varies from state to state. In many states the rule of thumb is that the income must be increased by at least 10% in order for the court to consider an increase in child support. If the absent parent receives only a 3.3% cost of living increase per year, in three years (and every three years) you will be able to petition the court for an increase in child support. If the absent parent gets a new job and is making 10% more than he or she was before, your child may be entitled to more support. Do remember that along with the absent parent's ability to pay an increased amount of support comes whether the additional money is needed. You must prove to the court that the money you are asking for on behalf of your children is something that they need. If you are simply asking for a "cost of living" increase every three years — that's one thing — but if you are seeking a modification due to *changed circumstances,* be prepared to prove your case in court. You may want to use the income versus expenses chart at the end of this chapter.

The absent parent receives an inheritance.

If you know of an inheritance that the absent parent has received or will be receiving, you may be able to seek an upward modification for a *change in circumstances* based on the absent parent's new ability to pay. For example: let's say that your child's doctor has recommended 36 months of speech therapy, but neither you nor the absent parent has been able to afford it. Your child's speech is getting worse and you are despairing. Suddenly, you find that your child's other parent has inherited a nice sum of money. You can then petition the court to have the absent parent pay the bill for the speech therapy since he or she can now afford it.

There is a rise in cost for caring for your children, as they grow older.

Children eat more, grow out of their clothes faster, and are involved in more activities, as they grow older. All of this requires more money. If it is a significant amount more, your circumstances may have changed and you should petition for an upward modification.

A new medical, mental, or emotional diagnosis is made, or your child becomes ill or disabled.

If you have increased expenses due to your child becoming temporarily or permanently ill or disabled in some way, you should petition the court for more financial support from the absent parent.

These are just a few reasons that an *upward modification*

can be granted. Use your discretion. You should always ask yourself two questions: Is the absent parent in a better paying position than they were when the child support award was granted? Is there a good reason for you to ask for more money on your child's behalf? Some changes in circumstances do not fit into any specific category so do not rule out situations that may seem unusual. For example: lottery winnings, a substantial change in either parents taxes, recommended private school for your child, etc. Also, be sure of your reasons for asking for additional child support. If you are still unsure about what is a change in income, there is more information in chapter nine. Before you get there however, there is a lot more that you need to know about modifications first.

How many times have you heard the saying — be careful of what you wish for — because you just may get it? That saying holds true when it comes to child support modifications. You may go to court expecting to get an *upward modification* only to have the decision-maker look over your paperwork, decide that you are getting too much money as it is, and lower your child support award! If that happens, you will end up with a modification, just not the type you expected. You must be properly prepared when you ask for a modification. You must also have good and significant reasons for receiving the amount of amount that your child(ren) get now, as well as any additional monies you are requesting.

It is not uncommon for the absent parent to petition the court for a *downward modification.*

Some of the situations that might call for a *downward modification* are:

The absent parent goes on disability.
The absent parent retires.
The absent parent loses his or her job or has his or her salary greatly reduced.

There are few reasons for a judge to grant a *downward modification.* The main one would be that the current child support order is too high to begin with or that there has been a change of circumstances and the children do not need as much money. For example: additional child support may have been written into the agreement so that your child could have orthodontic work done on his or her teeth. Now that the braces are off, the additional money is not needed.

An absent parent can not get a *downward modification* simply because he/she lost their job. While they may suffer a temporary setback and it may be difficult for them for a while, the law sees the change as a "temporary" condition. The child support payment must still be paid in full. A *downward modification* can only be made under permanent changed circumstances, in most cases. Occasionally, there are times when a judge may order a temporary modification due to changed circumstances but they are not the norm. These situations are difficult to discuss since they can vary greatly.

Changes in circumstances for the purpose of a downward modification can not be voluntary. They must be circumstances that are out of the absent parent's control. For example: An absent parent can not quit his/her job and then claim change of circumstances and request that the child support amount be lowered. Quitting their job was a voluntary action. An absent parent can not decide to take a lesser position in their company where they will be making less money and request that child support be lowered. Taking a lesser position was a voluntary action. An absent parent can not go back to school, sell their business, or take time off to "find themselves" if it means that they will request that child support be lowered. These are all voluntary actions. Absent parents can not voluntarily reduce their income and pay less child support.

If an absent parent loses his/her job (which is a temporary situation and therefore not qualified for a reduction in child support), and finds another job making 25% less than they did at the last job, they may now be eligible for a *downward modification*. An involuntary 25% reduction in salary is substantial enough for a decrease in child support. Now let's assume that the absent parent found another job making 5% less than they did at the last job. They would not be eligible for a reduction in child support because most people are able to absorb a 5% reduction in salary.

There are other things besides child support that should be written into your child support order that may not be. If they are — congratulations, apparently you had a caseworker or attorney that actually knew what they were doing. If not, and if you were not made aware of these items, then you had a caseworker or attorney not unlike any other. Don't despair. Lucky for you, you are reading a chapter on how to change your child support order to get what your child needs.

The first item that should be included in your order is health insurance. If the absent parent has health insurance available to him or her through their job, the law requires that parent to cover his or her children. If health insurance is not available to the absent parent, but is available to the custodial parent for a fee, then an *upward modification* is in order for health benefits for the children.

Life insurance is another item that should be included in your child support order. If the absent parent should become ill or unexpectedly pass away, your children would be left in the lurch for financial support. Life insurance can be purchased inexpensively in any state. Have it written into your child support order that the absent parent is required to maintain life insurance in the amount of (whatever amount is right for your particular circumstances — consult an insurance agent). The absent parent can either maintain the insurance themselves or you can have the child support order adjusted upward slightly so that you can purchase and maintain the insurance on their behalf.

If you believe that your child(ren) will be attending college, you will want the absent parent to contribute to the financing of their education. At the very least, the absent parent should be required to foot 50% of the bill minus whatever contribution your child(ren) will be making themselves by working or taking out loans, etc. If you child(ren) choose an expensive school and the absent parent can not afford it, he or she may not be required to pay. Take all of this into consideration.

You may be wondering if you have a child support award

that needs modification. The chart below will help you to determine your change in expenses from the initial entry of your child support order, (or the most recent change), to now. It is similar to the chart that you used in chapter one with a few slight changes. As with any chart or checklist in this book, you may want to photo copy it so that it can be used several times, as needed.

COMPARATIVE INCOME AND EXPENSES

	PRIOR	CURRENT	NET CHANGE
Rent/Mortgage			
Repairs			
Insurance			
Taxes			
Water/Sewer			
Electricity/Gas			
Telephone			
Garbage			
School Lunches			
Meals Eaten Out			
Clothing			
Laundry/ Dry Cleaning			
Medical Insurance			
Other Medical Costs			
Dental/Vision			
Prescriptions			
Other Drugs			
Car Payment			
Car Insurance			
Car Repair			
Bus/Train/Cab			
Baby-sitter			
Other Child Care			
School Tuition			
School Supplies			
Extra Activities			
Religious Affiliation			
Newspapers/Mags			
Total - This Page			

Books	_____	_____	_____
Barber/Beauty Shop	_____	_____	_____
Union Dues	_____	_____	_____
Retirement Fund	_____	_____	_____
Recreation	_____	_____	_____
Vacation	_____	_____	_____
Pets	_____	_____	_____
Gifts for others	_____	_____	_____
Parties	_____	_____	_____
Birthday/ Holiday Gifts	_____	_____	_____
Other	_____	_____	_____
Other	_____	_____	_____
Total - This Page	_____	_____	_____
Total - Previous Page	_____	_____	_____
TOTAL	_____	_____	_____

TOTAL NET CHANGE;
   CUSTODIAL PARENT   _____
TOTAL NET CHANGE;
   NON-CUSTODIAL PARENT_____

TOTAL NET CHANGE   _____
TOTAL NET CHANGE
   OF EARNINGS   _____
TOTAL NET CHANGE
   OF EXPENSES   _____
TOTAL CHILD SUPPORT
   NECESSARY   _____

     In order to complete this chart you may have to go through your checkbook, credit card statements and receipts for the past year and see where you have been spending your money. If you are anything like me, I also list events that my daughter or I have to attend, and appointments that we must keep, on my calendar.

For example: birthday parties, school fair, doctor visits, etc. Your appointment book may also have a wealth of information that you may be able to find. Make a habit of writing everything that you do down somewhere, and keeping your date books and calendars for 5 years. They are good reference materials.

Now that you have checked your facts, you are ready to file your petition to modify your child support order. Visit the clerk of the court that handled your divorce/paternity suit or child support order and ask for a Motion and Order to Show Cause, for the purpose of a Child Support Modification. The court clerk should have papers to give to you. If they do not, you can follow the example that follows (item #1) and create one yourself on a computer or typewriter. Just be sure to follow it to the letter and have someone to check it over for you for accuracy purposes. Once the form has been completed, either you or your attorney, if you have one, must sign it and file it with the clerk of the court. This merely means that you will give the papers to them. The clerk will then set a date for a *hearing*. This means that he/she will tell you the date that you must appear in court. You must arrange for a copy of your *motion* to be served (given to) the non-custodial parent. This must be done by either a private process server or by the sheriff. There is a fee for this and it is generally $15.00. Call your local sheriffs office and ask the about their procedures. If you choose to use a private process server you can find one in the yellow pages of your phone book. There is usually no fee to file your *motion* with the court.

You will be using the same case number that you were originally assigned when you opened your child support case. That case number will follow you all the way through until your child(ren) become of age and are no longer receiving child support. If you move out of state, however, your case number will then change. If you have moved out of state you must arrange for a certified copy of your divorce decree/paternity action/child support order to be filed in the court of the county of the state where you are now living. Call the clerk's office in the new county and ask whether your copies need to be certified and "authenticated" before you send them in, or if they need to be

MOTION AND ORDER TO SHOW CAUSE,
RE: MODIFICATION

IN THE CIRCUIT COURT OF THE STATE OF ANY STATE
FOR THE COUNTY OF ANY COUNTY

IN the Matter of the Child Support Order of:)
)

JANE DOE,   )
     Petitioner,   )
) MOTION AND ORDER TO
     and   ) SHOW CAUSE RE: MODIFICATION
) (Ex Parte)
JOHN DOE,   )
     Respondent   )

TO: John Doe
                 666 Deadbeat Lane
                 New York, N.Y. 11111

        YOU ARE HEREBY ORDERED to file a written appearance by Affidavit in answer to the Motion and Affidavit filed by the Petitioner within thirty (30) days of the date of service of certified copies of this Motion and Order and Affidavit upon you, to **SHOW CAUSE**, if any there be:

        1. Why the Child Support Order entered in the above-entitled Court should not be modified to increase the amount of child support to the Uniform Guidelines amount.

        2. If this matter is contested, why judgement should not be entered in favor of Petitioner for Petitioner's reasonable attorney fees and court costs incurred in connection herewith pursuant to ORS 107.135.

        IT IS FURTHER ORDERED that should Petitioner fail to file such a written appearance by Affidavit within the time specified herein-above, a **DEFAULT ORDER** shall be applied for by the moving party.

        DATED this _____ day of _____, 199_.

_____
CIRCUIT COURT JUDGE

IT IS SO MOVED:

_____
Your name
Your Street Address
Your City, State, Zip
Your phone

ITEM #1: MOTION IN ORDER TO SHOW CAUSE REGUARDING MODIFICATION

transferred directly from the court of the previous state to the new state. Procedures can differ from state to state and from county to county so be sure to call and ask for the proper procedures in your own state and county.

Once your decree/action/order has been transferred, you will receive a new case number. You can then file your *motion* and have the non-custodial parent served. Be sure to serve any public assistance agency that you may be receiving benefits from, as well. Those should be sent to the administrator. If you do not know who the administrator is, simply call and ask. There is more information on how public assistance works with child support in chapter 11.

Item #2 is an Affidavit in support of Motion to Modify Child Support. An *affidavit* is a written statement that you are telling the truth under oath and in the presence of God, about whatever it is you have to say. In this particular case, your affidavit (your written statement — item #2), is supporting (backing up) your motion (request) to modify (change) your support order. In other words, you have filed your request to change your child support order and get more money. Item #2 will prove to the decision-maker why the extra money is needed and that the non-custodial parent can afford to pay for it. You will want the decision-maker to be aware of all your expenses before your court date so that she/he can be better prepared for your particular case. By submitting item #2 it will show that you are well prepared, well informed, and are to be taken seriously.

Since child support awards are based largely upon the income of the non-custodial parent, you will want to have up to date information on his/her income and assets to present to the decision-maker for consideration. Depending on your energy level, commitment to in the modification of your child support, and your relationship with the non-custodial parent, there are a couple of different routes that you can take to determine income.

Choice #1: You can ask. Some non-custodial parents will be honest about what they have and what they earn. If the decision-maker determines that they should pay more, they will. Their

AFFIDAVIT IN SUPPORT OF MOTION
AND ORDER TO MODIFY JUDGEMENT

IN THE CIRCUIT COURT OF THE STATE OF ANY STATE
FOR THE COUNTY OF ANY COUNTY

In the Matter of the Marriage of:)
JANE DOE,   )   No. AS-4569
    Petitioner,   )
)   AFFIDAVIT IN SUPPORT
    and   )   OF MOTION AND ORDER
)   TO MODIFY JUDGEMENT
JOHN DOE,   )
    Respondent,   )
STATE OF ANY STATE   )
County of Any County   )

    I, Jane Doe, being first duly sworn on oath, do hereby depose and say that:

    1. I am the Petitioner in the above-entitled matter.

    2. A substantial change in circumstances has occurred since the date of entry of the Child Support Order between the two parties. The change in circumstances include, but are not limited to, the following:

(THIS IS WHERE YOU WILL DETAIL THE CHANGES IN CIRCUMSTANCES. LIST ALL OF THE CHANGES AND THE AMOUNT OF MONEY FOR EACH THAT YOU WILL NEED TO COVER THEM. AT THE END OF YOUR LIST YOU WILL TOTAL YOUR CHANGED EXPENSES AND LIST THE ADDITIONAL AMOUNT OF CHILD SUPPORT THAT YOU WILL NEED FROM THE NON-CUSTODIAL PARENT. USE AS MUCH SPACE AS YOU NEED.)

_____
Sign your name here

    SUBSCRIBED AND SWORN to before me this _____
day of _____, 199___.

_____
NOTARY PUBLIC FOR ANY STATE   My Commission expires: _____

ITEM #2: AFFIDAVIT IN SUPPORT OF MOTION AND ORDER TO MODIFY JUDGEMENT

honesty eliminates the need for you to take any further steps to get information about them.

Choice #2: You can ask. Some non-custodial parents will not be honest about what they have and what they earn. They may fear that the child support order will be increased and they do not want that to happen. Either they really are having trouble making ends meet and are not just "crying wolf," or they are just poor excuses for parents, maybe both. In this case it is up to you to decide what to do. You can move on to choice number 3 that does give you another option. However, do realize that it is not the friendliest of choices to make. If you move on to choice 3 you are setting the scene for animosity between the two of you and maybe your children as well. These are personal choices that will affect your life so make your decisions carefully. There are some non-custodial parents who do not deserve the consideration of choices number 1 and 2. In that case I encourage you to move straight to choice number 3.

Choice #3: *Subpoena* the information that you need from the non-custodial parent or his or her attorney. In this case, do not waste your time asking for information that you most likely will not get anyway. Go for the gusto and haul out the big guns. Item #3 is a Request for Production. In this document you are asking for records of any and all monetary involvement that the absent parent has had for the past 3 years. This will reveal anything and everything that you need to know. It may be helpful to serve this document along with a subpoena for him or her to appear at a certain location so that you may ask him or her questions as well. Yes! It's all legal, you do not need an attorney to do it, and the non-custodial must appear with the documents you request or face penalties. There is more information on how to properly file a subpoena and get the non-custodial parent to show his or her face, in chapter 11. For now, the REQUEST FOR PRODUCTION can be done by mail — requesting that the non-custodial parent submit the documents you request by a certain date to a certain place. You can have them sent to your home,

REQUEST FOR PRODUCTION

IN THE CIRCUIT COURT OF THE STATE OF ANY STATE
FOR THE COUNTY OF ANY COUNTY

In the Matter of the Marriage of:)
)
JANE DOE,   )
    Petitioner,   )
)   REQUEST FOR PRODUCTION
    and   )
)
JOHN DOE,   )
    Respondent,   )

TO: John Doe, Petitioner

Pursuant to ORCP 43, Petitioner hereby requests that Respondent produce and permit the party making this request to inspect and copy all documents described in this request by ____ _.m. on the ___ day of ____, 199_.

As used in this request, the term "Documents" means and includes, without limitation, the following whether printed or recorded or reproduced by hand, and draft, duplicates, carbon copies, or any other copies thereof: agreements, communications, correspondence, telegrams, memoranda, summaries or records of telephone conversations, summaries or records of personal conversations or interviews, diaries, graphs, reports, notebooks, statements, plans, drawings, sketches, maps, photographs, contracts, licenses, ledgers, books of account, vouchers, bank checks, charge slips, credit memoranda, receipts, audit papers, working papers, statistical records, cost sheets, loan files, drafts, letters, any marginal comments appearing on any documents, and all others writings or papers similar to any of the foregoing, including information maintained on computer media.

Documents requested are all those in your possession, or in the possession of your attorney, or under your control or available to you, specifically the following:

1. All federal and state income tax returns for the tax years _____ through _____, inclusive, and documents showing any estimated taxes paid for tax years for which tax returns have not yet been filed, for you, together with copies of all partnership information returns prepared by or on behalf of any partnership to which you belonged during the same period.

2. All federal and state income tax returns for the tax years _____ through _____, inclusive filed by any closely held corporation, limited partnership or other entity in which you have, or had, an interest.

3. Any list of personal property prepared by either party.

4. All documents reflecting your income from all sources from _____ to date, including, but not limited to, W-2's 1099's, wage statements and paycheck stubs.

5. All documents showing any interest you have in real or personal property, including deeds, contracts, vehicle registration, titles, bills of sale, and any other documents concerning any assets in which you have claim or may claim any interest.

6. All documents showing any existence and nature of any security interest in any

ITEM #3: REQUEST FOR PRODUCTION

asset owned by you or any asset in which you claim an interest, including, but not limited to, mortgages, trust deeds and security agreements.

7. All documents relating to the purchase of any real or personal property in which you have an interest, together along with any closing statements prepared in connection with the purchase by you of any interest in real property.

8. All tax statements on any real property, business interest, or personal property owned by either party.

9. All financial statements prepared by or for you during the preceding five (5) years and loan applications submitted by you or any entity in which you have an interest to any bank or other lending institution or insurance company in connection with any application for a loan from _____ to date.

10. All documents evidencing your ownership or interest in any general partnership, limited partnership or closely held corporation in which you owned an interest at any time from _____ to the present, or in which you now own an interest, including any buy and sell agreements, stock purchase agreements and partnership agreements.

11. All documents which reflect the amount, location, and value of any stocks or bonds owned either jointly or individually by you.

12. All documents which reflect the amount and location of any checking accounts, savings accounts, money markets, stock brokerage or other financial institution accounts or similar accounts on which your name appears, or has appeared, on which you are or were a signer, or on which you have had funds or securities on deposit, including periodic statements, canceled checks, check registers (and/or stubs), deposit records, passbooks, and certificates of deposit for the period _____ to date.

13. Records of all charge accounts, credit accounts, and lines of credit, including copies of all statements reflecting charges made and payments received on said accounts from the period _____ to date.

14. All policies of insurance on the life of either party, together with all records related thereto.

15. All receipts reflecting cash purchases to you from _____ to date.

16. List of all safe deposit boxes to which you have access, and a list of all the contents of any such safe deposit boxes.

17. All records of all trusts, estates, life estates or other property in which you have any beneficial interest whatsoever, including a remainder interest or contingent remainder interest.

18. All appraisals prepared by anyone for any real property in which either party has any interest.

19. Any and all stock option or stock benefits between you and your employer, and any information concerning receipt of such stock for the past five(5)years.

20. All documents concerning any pension, profit sharing, retirement, vacation, savings, PERS, IRA, SEP, KEOUGH, 401k, Social Security, veteran's benefits, deferred compensation, or other similar plans, programs or accounts (past or present), including any and all statements reflecting your interest therein, any summary description of the plan, a copy of the plan, the name and address of the trustee, custodial and/or plan administrator or other officer in charge of each account or plan.

21. All records reflecting all income received by _____(husband, wife, girlfriend, boyfriend) from all sources, from _____ to date.

22. All records relating to any expenses or sums paid by you for which you have received reimbursement from your private practice, or your _____ association/employment with _____.

23. All records of all trusts, estates, life estates, or any other property in which you have any beneficial interest whatsoever, including a remainder interest or a contingent

ITEM #3: REQUEST FOR PRODUCTION, CON'T.

remainder interest, including, but not limited, to any Last Will and Testament, Codicil or other instrument or bequest which names you as a beneficiary or contingent beneficiary.

24. Your current last Will and Testament, together with any Codicils related thereto.

25. All stock certificates, bonds, indentures or any other security in which you claim an interest of any kind.

26. All health, medical, accident, hospital and dental insurance policies covering you or any member of your family.

27. All records reflecting any indebtedness that you owe, including, but not limited to, notes and contracts.

28. Any records reflecting any guarantee made by either party.

29. All documents or correspondence concerning any credit extended by you or any debt owed to you by anyone.

30. All documents concerning any benefits available to you under any programs, Social Security, veteran's benefits or any other program, private or public, under which you may have a claim for future payments of any kind or nature.

31. All documents listing, describing or showing the existence of personal property, jewelry, gold, silver, precious metals, gems, artwork, antiques, coins, stamp collections, or other similar assets in which you claim an interest,

32. Copies of all documents showing the existence of any lawsuit or claim against you or your spouse or by you or your spouse against any person or entity.

33. All documents showing any gifts, transfers or sales made by you of any asset with a value in excess of $500.00 during the preceding 36 months.

34. All documents showing the existence or describing any furniture, fixtures, office equipment or other similar assets owned by you.

35. All documents showing any farm implements, farm or logging equipment, tools or other equipment or machinery owned by you or in which you claim an interest,

36. All records showing any interest held by you in any livestock, horses, or any animal and all documentation showing the value thereof.

37. All documents showing any interest you have in any patent, trademark, copyright, royalty or other intangible asset.

38. All powers of attorney executed by you during the preceding three(3) years.

39. All documents of any kind or nature showing the existence or value of any asset of any kind or nature in which you claim any interest whatsoever.

****

This request is a continuing request. If the documents requested above come into to the possession or control of you or your attorneys after the date requested for the production herein, Petitioner requests that they be produced at the time of their availability.

DATED this _____ day of _____, 1994.

_____

Your Name
Your Street Address
Your City, Your State, Your Zip
Your Phone

ITEM #3: REQUEST FOR PRODUCTION, CON'T.

office or attorneys' office — wherever you choose.

When your court date comes, the non-custodial parent or his/her attorney will most likely object to a modification. Because you will have already done a "discovery"— a "sneak preview" look at the documents that will be shown in court — (your request for production) — there will not be too much information that he/she can dispute. After all you asked for information concerning all of his/her money matters, and that's what you got. They cannot possibly dispute information that they gave you. The most that they can say is that your expenses are too high or that there has not been a significant enough of a change to warrant an upward increase in child support. This is why it is important for you to be able to prove your case.

When you have your day in court you may have an opportunity to speak. If you will be nervous, as most people are, you may want to bring this prepared speech with you. Look the decision-maker in the eye and say:

"Your honor, (if the decision-maker is a judge) or Ms./ Mr. _____ (their name should be on a name plate on the desk in front of them. If it is not, ask who will be hearing your case before the hearing begins) I have filed an affidavit with the court that I am prepared to testify to. The information in my affidavit is the information I wish the court to rely upon. If you should have any questions for me, I will be happy to answer them, otherwise I have no further information to provide."

At this point it is up to the decision-maker to decide whether to increase your support or not. If you have gone over the expenses versus income chart with a fine toothed comb and it shows that you are due for an increase, then you have a good chance of getting one.

Although most of these procedures are typically done through attorneys, as I mentioned before, you do not have to have an attorney to get your modification. Just follow the simple directions that have been outlined for you and you should do just fine.

If you are considering hiring an attorney however, the following three chapters should help you in your search. Attorneys are fine to work with if they do not charge you an arm and a leg, which most of them do — and if they really know about child support enforcement ... which most family law attorneys do not. They do have their good points. Decide for yourself if one is good for you.

Chapter 5: Hiring A Private Attorney

The first thing that most people consider when they are trying to collect child support is finding and hiring an attorney. Having an attorney can make your life a hell of a lot easier since they can negotiate the child support system on your behalf. On the other hand, an attorney can also make your life a living hell if they do not know how to handle child support enforcement cases correctly. You can pay an attorney to work for you if you can afford it, you can find an attorney to work for you for free if you are *indigent,* or you can pursue your child support case *"pro se' "* (without an attorney). This chapter will deal with hiring a private attorney that you must pay, and some methods that can be used to creatively pay their fee.

If you are going to hire an attorney to collect child support money that's past due, your best bet would be to find a small law firm that specializes in the collection of debts. Attorneys that work for large firms usually will want to work with matters that can make them a lot of money or bring them a lot of prestige. Unless the amount of money that your child(ren) is owed is the mid to high five figures, at least, chances are that a large firm will not want to work with you since it will not be beneficial to them. There are firms however, that specifically hire collection attorneys. That is, attorneys that are trained to collect debts from people that owe money. Typically, these attorneys get their clients from companies that are owed money. After a few letters are sent requesting the money that is due, these companies send the bills to an attorney to collect the money for them. People who owe money will usually respond to a letter from an attorney because they are afraid of legal action. If they do not pay the bill immediately, the attorney then can file a lawsuit against the person or company that owes the money.

Begin by looking in the yellow pages of your phone book under collection agencies. Call all of the collection agencies that are listed and ask them for the name of their collection attorney because you would like to hire him or her. When you have a list of at least 10 attorneys, call them all. It's important to call more than just a few since they will quote different fees to you. Some may not be willing to work with you, and those that will work with you will all charge different fees.

It is not advisable to work with your cousin the real estate attorney, or your best friend's father, the criminal attorney, even though you know they have your best interest at heart. Law is a learned trade. The criminal attorney has spent his time learning criminal law, and the real estate attorney has spent his time learning real estate law. Family law attorneys have spent their time learning family law (which child support falls under), but they may not know how to get it collected once it's due.

If you are unable to find an attorney through collection agencies in your area, the next best bet is to call small firms in your area that specialize in "general law." General law means that they are a jack of all trades and will take any case as long as it will make them money and they believe that they can handle it. These small firms work well because they work hard, and it's cases like yours that are the meat and potatoes of their business. If they do not know something, generally they will persist until they get the information that they need to help you.

Remember that you should have a good relationship with your attorney. You should not feel as if someone is putting you down or doing you a favor by taking your case. You are paying them good money to do a job. If you feel at any time during your interview that your chemistry is not "right," or if you believe that they are not capable of helping you, do not hire them.

Attorney fees vary from firm to firm and from state to state. Generally, you will be billed an hourly fee unless other arrangements are made in advance. If you do not have the money to pay an attorney up front for their services, you can try a little bit of "creative financing." Not all attorneys will go for this so it is up to you to express your enthusiasm and confidence in your case and why the attorney should be willing to work unconventionally. The following questions should be asked:

Question #1: Ask if they are willing to take the case on a contingency basis. Contingency means that if they do not collect any money for you then they are not paid. Usually accident cases work this way. The law firm pays all the expenses that are necessary to try the case or get a settlement. When the money is recovered, they take a percentage of the total amount. The percentage that they take can vary greatly, but it is usually about a third of the total that is won. For example, if the child support amount that is outstanding is $10,000, then your attorney's law firm would end up with $3,333, and your child(ren) would get $6,667. That's a huge chunk of money to lose out on, so you would have to make the hard decision of whether it is worth it to you or not. Some people take the opinion that it is not worth it since the money that is being lost rightfully belongs to their child(ren) and should not come out of their pocket. Others hold the position that if they are not getting any money for their children now and have had to go to an attorney to enforce their child support order, then chances are that unless some drastic action is taken, the child support money will never be recovered. In this instance it is rationalized that a little bit of money is better than none at all. Only you on behalf of your children can make these difficult choices for your own family.

If you do find an attorney that is willing to take the case on a contingency basis, do not be surprised if they want more than a third. They may ask you for 40% or 50% of what is owed. Why? Because they know you are in a difficult position and may have no where else to turn. Another reason for charging a lot is because child support cases can be difficult to work. Only you can decide if it's worth it to you.

Question #2: Another option you have is to ask if they are willing to put you on a payment plan to work off your debt to them. Often, attorneys are willing to make this type of arrangement. If you are really strapped for cash as most custodial parents are especially when they are not getting child support, you may not be able to pay anything to an attorney. It is an option to consider if you have money to lay out.

The key to both of these options, whether they may work for you, is the amount of child support that is past due. Obviously, if you go to an attorney and ask for a contingency plan when your child(ren) are owed $3,000 in past due child support, the plan would not work for you in most cases. The law firm in this case would only stand to make $1,000. While $1,000 may be a lot to some people, the average attorney would scoff at that amount considering the headaches they may endure while attempting to collect the money. And they only get paid if they are successful. Also consider the part of the country that you live in. In the Northeast $1000 does not get you very far, while in the Midwest the value is a lot greater.

After you have discussed contingency fees and payment plans and are making an appointment to see your potential attorney, before you end your conversation there are other things that you need to know. Find out if they charge a consultation fee for the time that it takes to meet with you. Some attorneys charge consultation fees and you need to know this before you make your appointment. If they do charge such a fee, you need to know how much. Some law firms also require a *retainer*. A *retainer* is a fee paid to an attorney when the client (that's you) hires them. It's a deposit that is applied towards the fees that you will be charged.

Now that we are clear on some of the benefits and drawbacks of hiring a private attorney, let's move on to how you can find an attorney to work for you at no charge or dirt cheap!

Chapter 6: Finding A Free Attorney

After reading Chapter 5, "Hiring a Private Attorney," you now know that there are many creative ways of paying your attorney once you decide to hire them. The attorney that you choose has to be agreeable to it, of course. You will now learn ways of getting an attorney to work for you for absolutely nothing at all. Absolutely nothing out of your pocket that is, and that is what we are concerned about, right?

Nothing is for free. Everything must be paid for. This does not mean that you have to be the one who pays. If you have tried to hire a private attorney but can not afford one the conventional way, and you have not found one that will work with you creatively concerning payment, you can try one or all of these next four suggestions:

LEGAL AID:

Attorneys are available for custodial parents who are trying to get child support from an absent parent. Usually, every county in every state will have an office to serve you. If you do not know where the legal aid office in your area is, you may:

1. Call information from your home telephone. Ask them for the legal aid office in your county. In most areas an information call will cost more money than a regular local call would. If you do not want to pay the extra money because you are on a tight budget, as most custodial parents are, use a public pay phone to place the information call. Most pay phones will not charge you for an information call. Then go home and place the local call from your home telephone.

2. Look it up in your phone book. In the white page portion of your telephone book, search for a listing under Legal Aid. In the yellow page portion, look under both "attorneys" and "lawyers" and then search for any listing under Legal Aid. There may also be an advertisement. Be sure to look at those as well. You can also check the blue pages under government agencies in your county. A telephone number for legal aid may be listed there.

3. Call your local welfare department or child support enforcement agency. Tell them that you are searching for your county's legal aid office. Generally, they should be able to help you.

4. Your local library has a wealth of information. Call or visit the reference desk and let the reference librarian know that you need to find the legal aid office for your area. If anyone can find the number and address in a flash, the reference librarian can.

In order to use the services of the legal aid office you must be either indigent or have an income that is considered to be on or below the poverty level for where you live. If you are on welfare you will automatically qualify for services. If you have a job but make very little money, you need to find out what the poverty level is in your area to know whether you qualify or not. A large number of people fall into a gray area that is sometimes difficult to determine. There are some people that may not be on welfare, or have a job, they may not be getting child support for their children, but because they own the house that they live in — they will not qualify for free legal services. Some people do not have any source of income, and are not receiving court ordered child support or alimony, yet they have been forced to leave their homes with their children because they can no longer afford the upkeep. They still may not be qualified for legal aid because they are still married to their spouse who is a high earner. Therefore, it is thought that they do not need handouts. There are many situations such as these where custodial parents are turned down for legal assistance even though they have no money of their own. If this sounds like your situation, you must prepare your financial statement before your appointment with the legal aid office. Use the chart that is available to you in Chapter 1 "Establishing your child support order." It will help you to outline what your expenses are. You will also need to provide the legal aid office with information on all of your income, including child support and alimony, if you get any. You need to show that even though you may have a spouse that makes a great deal of money, he or she does not give you any. Bring your overdue bills, eviction notices and whatever else you have to plead your case. If you do have assets, ask if they will place a lien on your property to be paid when the property is sold and the proceeds are divided between you and your spouse. There is more information on liens and how they can work to your advantage in Chapter 10. Although the legal aid office has guidelines that they follow when they accept clients, they will make their own final decision.

When you use the services of the legal aid office, if it is shown that you have no money to pay your bill, as in the case of indigence, you will receive the services free of charge. If it is thought that you are not completely indigent, you may be asked to pay a reduced fee. Normally this is billed, according to your income, on a sliding scale. The more money that you make, the more that you will be charged, up to the normal fee that others pay. The less money you make, the less you will be charged. If you are planning to use the services of a legal aid office, keep in mind that they usually have a long waiting list. If you qualify for free or reduced rate services, put your name on the waiting list anyway. If something else comes up in the meantime, in which you are able to get an attorney by other means, then it's just gravy for you. You need to have as many choices as you can. Do not worry about not needing their services when your time comes; it will be easy for them to go on to the next person on the list.

BAR ASSOCIATION:

Every state has a Bar Association from which you can get attorney referrals. Simply find the telephone number to the Bar Association in your state by using the same methods described in the section on legal aid. Place your call and ask that you be referred to a few attorneys that specialize in child support cases. If they do not have any attorneys with that specialty, ask for attorneys that specialize in divorce or family law. Ask for a child support attorney since not all divorce or family law attorneys know how to enforce a child support order. You also want attorneys that are willing to collect their fee from the non-custodial parent, or that are willing to place a lien on your property instead of receiving any up front payment.

There may not be any information listed with the Bar Association other than what type of law each attorney practices. It's worth a shot to mention it. Some Bar Associations have more information than others. If they do not have the information that you need you may have to call each attorney that you are referred to and ask them yourself. The Bar Association will usually refer you to three or four attorneys at a time. They also may charge a fee; ask them up front if they do, then decide if you still wish to use their service.

GOVERNMENT ATTORNEYS:

Government attorneys are free to anyone and everyone who wants to use them — with a few catches, however. They are usually referred to as *Title IV-D* attorneys because they work for the *IV-D* agencies. *IV-D* agencies are the child support enforcement agencies in every county that are bound by law to help you enforce your child support order. This is the office that you visit when you open your child support case. If you have a case that is easy to manage the caseworker that you have been assigned to may be the only person with which you have contact. If your case is in need of more legwork ... if the non-custodial parent needs to be located, or if you need a wage withholding, etc., a government attorney will have to be the one to handle these matters for you. The attorney will only become involved if certain services need to be implemented. The attorney is free and is available to anyone who has a case in an IV-D agency. This is not an attorney that you can call up and hire as you would any other. They are sheltered and protected by the agency because there are not many of them. They have an overwhelming caseload and have a difficult time keeping up with the many cases that they are assigned. Frankly, publicizing their existence is sure to cause problems for them and a longer waiting list for you. The reason I am willing to cause such a ruckus is because no one at the agency will tell you about them unless they are forced to do so. This does not help you in the least bit. What does help you, is knowing that there are things that these attorneys can do that can make a world of difference to your child support case. They will be covered in more detail in chapter 12, "What the government can do for you." As with any other attorney or other goods or services that you can get for free, it will not be made easy for you. First you must again put yourself on the waiting list, or at least let it be known that you want and need the services of these attorneys. You will be fully prepared after reading this entire book to inform the attorney of what services you feel will work well with your case. You can then ask if they have any further suggestions. You will be attempting to build a relationship with this attorney so that the two of you can work together to enforce your child support order. One bit of caution: Since these are government attorneys they work for the government and they do not work for you. Uncle Sam hires them to help collect on cases in which the government is particularly interested. If you are on welfare the government is supporting you so they have a direct interest in whether you get your child support or not. Every child support case of those who are on welfare is handled by the state collection agencies — the Title *IV-D* child support enforcement offices that I have been referring to. If you have read the introduction to this book, you know that when these agencies were opened in 1974 the government decided to give the same services to anyone who had a child support case. So even though these attorneys primary interest is not in helping the non-welfare cases, they will. Just remember that they do not work directly for you. It will be awfully difficult to fire them and you may not want to since they have the goods to help you. One more final word — anything you share with them will be shared with the government as well. There will not be any client confidentiality in your relationship as far as the government is concerned. Also, you will be sharing your attorney with many others. If the non-custodial parent of your child has another child by someone else, you may have to share your attorney with him or her as well.

If you contact your local office for assistance from a government attorney you are likely to get one or more of these responses:

    A. You may be told to retain a private attorney
    B. You may be discouraged from seeking assistance from a government attorney due to a long waiting list
    C. You may be told that you can not contact the government attorney; they will contact you
    D. You may be told that there aren't any government attorneys
    E. People may be rude to you and not help you at all

If you get any of these responses, and chances are good that you will, do not let them confuse or anger you. Read on, in the chapter titled "Effective Complaining" you will learn how to deal with these issues.

NON-CUSTODIAL PARENT PAYS ATTORNEY FEES:

If you must take the non-custodial parent to court to collect our child support, you can normally collect attorney fees from them. If, after reading this entire book, you decide that it may be in your best interest to go to court, you will possibly be in a better position to hire an attorney without any payment from you. Most judges will award attorney fees to the plaintiff (that's you) and attorneys know this. The drawback is that the amount awarded to you may be significantly lower than the fee you will be charged. This is where some more creative financing may have to come into play. Your attorney may not ask you for the remainder of the bill, but if she or he does you will be responsible for it.

The non-custodial parent may scoff at your attorney bill. If you are not able to collect child support, chances are that you will not be able to get this bill paid either. On the other hand, after appearing in court the non-custodial parent may come to his or her senses. Maybe, or maybe not. This advice may not help all custodial parents but it will give some of you another option — for others — it will actually work. If it does not help you, just press on. At the very least, you have just added more money onto the bill that the non-custodial parent can not run away from forever. For now — maybe. Forever — never.

Chapter 7: When Hiring An Attorney: Things To Know

"The first thing we do, first let's kill all the lawyers."
— William Shakespeare (Henry VI)

I used to date a fellow who walked very heavily. He nearly stomped everywhere he went. One day his father, who was sick of him stampeding throughout the house, yelled, "You better grow up to be a lawyer because you damn sure walk like one!"

Most lawyers are arrogant, abrasive, and think that they know everything. They have a superior attitude and make a living intimidating non-lawyers into paying large sums of money for their advice which adds up to nothing more than good research done at the law library. It is for this reason that I believe you do not absolutely need a lawyer to enforce your child support order. (On the other hand, they are arrogant and have feelings of superiority because they have spent three years in law school learning methods of intimidation so that they can go to court to win cases for their clients.) Dealing with lawyers is a mixed blessing. There are good sides to having a hired legal gun, and there are some downsides as well. As long as you know both sides of the coin, you can decide what will work out better for you.

If you are considering going to the law firm of "Do We Cheat 'Em And How" to hire a lawyer, there are some things that you should know. First of all, you are hiring him/her for his/her expertise and this means two things:

Fact #1: You are the boss. Your lawyer may know how to work the legal system, she/he may have taken a course on intimidation 101, and they may be able to muddle through the paperwork easier than you can. The key word is, "hire". You are hiring the lawyer, you are paying the lawyer. You are the boss. Your boss may have hired you for your expertise in the job that you do, but she/he is your boss. She/he sees to it that you are paid. If she/he is not happy with the job that you are doing she/he is sure to let you know. They may even fire you, if necessary. You need to take the same attitude with the lawyer you hire. You are the boss. If you do not like the services that you are receiving, be sure to let your "employee know." If worst comes to worst, you can fire your lawyer and get another one. We will get back to that later.

Fact #2: Your "expert" may not be an expert at all. Just because someone has attended law school does not mean that they are a good lawyer; it also does not mean that they can effectively practice any type of law. If you were a pregnant woman, whom would you go to — an obstetrician or a cardiologist? If you had a choice, you would probably go to the obstetrician, because they are the ones who have been trained in medical school to help deliver healthy babies. A cardiologist could probably deliver a baby too, if they had to, most doctors could. An obstetrician, however, has been specifically trained to help pregnant women. It's the same with lawyers. Most lawyers could practice any kind of law if they had to. All they would have to do is spend a few days in the law library doing some research and most people would never know the difference. The majority of lawyers, however, do have some kind of specialty. There are real estate lawyers, construction lawyers, malpractice lawyers, etc. Of course you will want a lawyer that practices family law. Just because a lawyer is a family law specialist, does not mean that they are good at what they do. You will want to interview any lawyer before you hire them. To that end, here is a list of questions that you will want to ask any lawyer before you allow them take your case:

   1. Are they experienced with enforcing child support orders? You will want to know what methods they have used to get non-custodial parents to pay. There are many methods that can be used, so basically you will be tap dancing on their head to see how many they can come up with and regurgitate to you in about 5-10 minutes. The next few chapters detail most of the methods. After you finish reading this book, you will know what to look for. Obviously, the attorney that is up to speed, in terms of knowledge, will be an attorney you are interested in.
   2. Of course, you are still interested in financing your attorney. You will want to know: how much they charge, is there a consultation fee, do they want a retainer, will they work on a contingency fee, will they take a payment plan? The attorneys that you will be interested in, are the ones who will agree to work with you in some way.
   3. Are they subscribers to any *credit reporting agencies*? The attorney that you select may need to use the *credit reporting agencies* to gather information about the non-custodial parent. If they are subscribers to the agencies, which means that they pay them a monthly fee to have access to credit reports, it will be easier for them to get the information. If they are not subscribers, they will have to go to another attorney, pay them a fee and ask them to get the information for them. Obviously it will be easier and cheaper, if they could get the information directly. There is more on how credit reports can be used to your advantage in Chapters 8 -11.
   4. Will they be willing to obtain liens and judgements against the non-custodial parent on your behalf? Are they familiar

with how to have a wage execution implemented? Will they issue subpoenas and conduct judgement debtor exams for you? (Do not worry about what these things mean right now, you will find out in the upcoming chapters.) Chances are you will get a few raised eyebrows when you ask these questions. The lawyer that you will be interviewing will probably be wondering where you got all of this information. Of course you will be able to answer any questions that she/he ask of you, intelligently, because you will have read this entire book and you will have the answers needed. If you can not remember everything, bring the book with you. The important thing is that you are investigating to select the right attorney to handle your case. That will earn you some respect.

5. Asking for references is another good way of judging whether a particular attorney will be good for you or not. Ask for a list of three clients that the attorney has already helped and be sure to speak with all three referrals. If you are not able to get into contact with them all, call the attorney back and ask for others. When you call the references that the attorney has given to you, do not bother to ask if she/he was a good attorney. Chances are the reference was satisfied with the work that was done for them, or the attorney would not have given you their name in the first place. What you are going to ask will be more specific. Inquire of the procedures the attorney used and if they were a pleasure to work with or not. If the attorney that you are considering uses mostly standard procedures and is not very innovative, they will not be a good choice for you. Likewise, if they possess many characteristics that typically cause clients to be discontented with their attorneys then you may want to continue to look. Some of these characteristics are:

A. Failure to return phone calls
B. Failure to file documents on time
C. Charging too much money
D. Not doing what they have promised to do
E. Being late for appointments or court dates

The best way to be referred to an attorney is through someone who has used her/him before. If you know someone that has been divorced, ask if they liked their attorney and why. Find out if they had any of the detrimental characteristics listed above.

Before you choose an attorney, you should have spoken with at least 10 of them and gotten references on at least 5. (When you have at least 3 attorneys that you liked over the phone, checked their references, and it seems that you will be able to work with them, make appointments to meet with them). This will be the interview portion that was mentioned before. This is the last step before selecting the attorney that you will want to work with you. Begin by writing down a list of questions that you will want to ask this attorney. When you meet with her/him be confident, be professional, be relaxed. It may be helpful for you to bring a pad or notebook with you, so you can jot down information that you want to remember. After you have met with your three prospective choices, choose the one that you feel will best represent you and with whom you can be a working partner. Also to consider: Choose an attorney that works in the same county, if not the same town, where your case will be heard. The reasons for this are simple. First, chances are that if your attorney works in the same town or county, they have what is known as the "home court advantage." (When sports teams play on their home court, they always feel more empowered and more of their fans are there to cheer them on to victory). It's the same on the legal court. The home court attorney may know the other attorneys in the courtroom and they may even know the judge. They may be able to talk to the judge and relate to her/him in a way that a stranger could not. When possible, and when it makes sense, always go with the home court advantage. Second, if your attorney has to travel distances to appear in court on your case, you are going to pay extra fees.

When all is said and done, if you find yourself with a bad attorney, fire her/him. It is not uncommon for clients to switch attorneys in the middle of a case, so do not be ashamed to do it. Just call her/him and explain that you would like to have your case file forwarded to your new attorney and then give her/his name. If you are asked for an explanation you may give one if you so choose, but it is not required. If you are too uncomfortable making the call, your new attorney will be happy to do it for you.

Chapter 8: Locating The Obligor

When I was a girl of about ten I read mystery novels in which a teenage sleuth would solve problems in her town. I was fascinated with how the young detective would have the smallest clues and yet was able to solve her mysteries. This chapter reminds me of my childhood with that young detective. Most custodial parents with child support orders will find that, at some point, they may either need to search for the non-custodial parent, or their assets or sometimes both. The smallest of offenders may move to a different town or county or maybe take a new job and not advise you. This makes it difficult to get money from them. The larger offenders will go through a lot more trouble. It is not uncommon for those who owe child support (*obligors*) to move to a new state. They may also put all of their assets into their new spouses name, lie and cheat on tax documents, and more, all in the name of not paying child support. That is why this chapter was written. Countless numbers of child support cases are left untouched in the child support agencies, simply because the case workers do not have enough information. They cannot find the obligors or they believe that they do not have jobs or that they earn far less than they actually do. Unless they have more information, their hands are tied. If you want your child support you may have to put on your own detective caps and get to work. Information that can be used to track someone down is abundant, you just have to know where to look.

When I was in college and I had my first apartment, I worked at a bank collecting on loans that were past due. Frequently, I had accounts where the customer skipped town without paying their bill. These accounts were called "skips". Part of my job was to perform preliminary "skip tracing" on these accounts before they were sent to our legal department. During my employment at that bank I was honored for being the "Collector of the Month" in my department every month that I was there. I will now share some of my secrets with you.

The first thing you want to do is gather as much information about the obligor that you can. If you lived with him or her you may have more information at your disposal than someone who did not. If you are still living with the obligor, or have access to his or her personal financials, you are ahead of the game. Photocopy whatever paper work you can, especially income tax records for the past 3 to 5 years and the obligors' social security number. Brainstorm for any information that you can come up with. When you are done, get paper and a pen to list the answers to the following data:

1. What is the obligor's full name? Has he/she ever used any other names? Does he/she have any nicknames.
2. What is the obligor's birth date? Where were they born?
3. What is the obligor's social security number?
4. What is the most recent address that you have for the obligor?
5. List the addresses that the obligor has had for the past 3 years.
6. What is the most recent telephone number that you have for the obligor?

7. Where does the obligor work? Write down the name of the company as well as the address and telephone number. Do you know his/her supervisor's or manager's name? Write it down. What does the obligor do for a living; what is his/her title?
8. List the obligor's employers for the past 3 years, as well as their addresses and phone numbers. Also list the supervisor or manager. Was he/she employed in the same capacity as they are now?
9. If the obligor is self employed list the clients that he/she has had for the past 3 years. If you have their addresses and/or telephone numbers, list those as well.
10. What is the obligor's State and Drivers License Number? What is the Make, Model, and Year of the vehicle that he/she drives? What is the plate number and the VIN (vehicle identification number)?
11. Has the obligor been formally married? If so, list all former marriages including the dates of the marriage and dissolution. List the former spouse's maiden name and their employment histories as well.
12. List the names and addresses and the obligor's parents, include the obligor's mother's maiden name. If they still work, what are their occupations and where are they employed?
13. List the obligor's siblings and friends along with their addresses, telephone numbers, and employment info.
14. List the obligor's creditors.
15. List the obligor's bank and Insurance Company.
16. List any real estate that the obligor owns.
17. Does the obligor belong to any clubs or organizations? List them.
18. What hobbies does the obligor have?
19. Does the obligor vote? If so, where are they registered and what party do they vote for?
20. Does the obligor receive, or will the obligor receive in the future any military, government or private pension or other benefits?

21. List any military service of the obligor. Include the branch of service, dates and locations of assignment, rank, service #, date and status of discharge.
22. If the obligor has ever been in prison list the conviction(s) including the date and location of conviction, the offense and location of incarceration.
23. If the obligor is or has ever been on probation, list the state and county and the name of the probation officer.
24. Is the obligor presently married? If so, assemble all of the before mentioned information on their spouse as well.

Along the way you will undoubtedly uncover other information that you could not put your hands on or did not know about the obligor from the start. Add what you find out to your reference. The more that you know about your obligor, the better your chances are of locating him or her. It's like a game of hide and seek. Your obligor is hiding and you're going to find him. Now that you have your completed list I will tell you how to use it. Ready? COME OUT, COME OUT, FROM WHEREVER YOU ARE!

TELEPHONE DIRECTORIES

The simplest way to locate anyone is through a telephone directory. Although it may sound foolish – why on earth would anyone who is trying to hide have a listed telephone number – it's not uncommon. So just to be certain that you are covering all of your bases you should call the information bureau in your area. Ask for the obligor by name in the city that you have last known him or her to live. Be sure to also check under any other names that the obligor may be using. Every name that the obligor has ever used is suspect. If you are able to get a telephone number ask if there is an address listed as well. Some information directories will give you an address if they have one, some will not. In some areas there is an address directory that can be used if you have a telephone number. It is an automated system that is used by punching in the telephone number of the person that you would like to have an address for. If the person has not given permission for his or her address to be publicly listed, you will be given the address that they have available. In the N.Y. Metropolitan area the number is address directory is 555-5454. Ask the telephone information bureau in your area if there is such a service that you can use.

Most likely you will get one of these two responses: You may find that there is a listing for your obligor, but that the telephone number is not available to the public. If this is the response that you are given press on, you will be able to utilize other methods in this chapter to locate an address now that you know that the obligor is in town. There is also the possibility that you will get a listed number and call it only to find that the number you received has been reassigned to someone else and that it is not a correct number after all. The smallest possibility remains that you could actually get a real working number for the obligor, but let's not bet the bank on it.

BACKWARD DIRECTORIES

When I was working in collections there were times that we were able to find a current telephone number for an obligor, but no address. Conversely maybe we had an address, but no telephone number. When this situation occurred we had special directories to help us out. There are several companies that make these directories. In our office we used "Coles" directories and "Backward" directories. They are just what they sound like, backward listings of telephone numbers and addresses. In these directories you can look up a persons telephone number and find their address. Likewise, you can use their address to find a telephone number. These directories can be found at your local library, the reference librarian should be able to show you how to use them. If your library doesn't have them because they are too small to stock such items, go to the largest library in your area they will be sure to carry at least one brand. Also available are "City Directories" at the local Chamber of Commerce. These City Directories give the same information, with one additional plus: it may also state the found persons occupation and place of employment. City Directories are mainly used to obtain current addresses for the service of legal documents. Since that is what you need it for, it should work perfectly for you.

These directories will also provide names, addresses and telephone numbers of neighbors or former neighbors of the obligor. Continue on with this chapter and you will find out why this information can be helpful to you.

POST OFFICE

It used to be very easy to get information from the post office. Years ago anyone could walk into a post office and get the forwarding address of someone that had moved. In fact it was far too easy. Men who beat up, threatened and stalked their wives and girlfriends would easily get this information and follow their ex's to their new address and continue the same patterns of abuse. Sadly, sometimes these women would end up being killed because of it. Because of this the Domestic Violence Act was put into place. You can no longer get information from the post office unless you have a valid legal reason for having it, and you must be able to prove it. The only exception to this rule is for attorneys and law enforcement. If you are an attorney (or have one working for you) or someone involved in law enforcement and you are tracing someone, the post office will give you the information that you request without a problem. For our purposes you must prove that you need the new address to serve legal documents on the person you are looking for.

Your first step is to obtain a judgement against the obligor. If you have already been to court and have received a court order for child support but the obligor is not paying, that is enough. When someone at the post office asks for proof that you will be serving legal documents, supply your child support order and the motion that you will be serving. Having a judgement is the easiest way to prove that you have a valid legal reason to have the obligor's new address. If you need the address to take the obligor to court for the first time your task becomes a bit more difficult. There is almost no way to prove that you will be using the address within the realms of the law. You may have to serve him or her "by

66

publication".

This is described later in this chapter.

If you are able to prove that you have legal reasons for needing the obligor's address you can request the information two ways: 1. The easiest and the fastest way to get the information you need is to go directly to the post office in the area where the obligor last received mail. Bring your documentation with you and expect to pay a small fee of about $5.00. The postal clerk will ask you to fill out a "Freedom of Information" form which they will provide to you. They will do an immediate search and give you the obligor's new address on the spot. 2. If you are unable to go to the post office you can ask that a Freedom of Information form be mailed to you. You can then fill it out attach your documentation, the appropriate fee and mail it back in to the post office. They in turn will reply to you by mail within about 30 days. If you do not want to waste valuable time you can create a Freedom of Information form yourself (see item#4), fill it out and mail it to the post office.

If the obligor was receiving mail at a post office box the postal clerk will be able to get the address from the application that the obligor completed when the box was rented. If the post office box was rented under a business name the information contained on the application is considered to be public knowledge. You will not have to prove legal reasons for wanting the renters address so you can get this information by visiting the post office, by mail, and even over the telephone.

Often you will find that deadbeat obligors move around quite a bit. Once you have received a new address it doesn't guarantee that the obligor still lives there. If you want to know up front whether the obligor still lives at the address that the post office is supplying to you, simply add to your form another line: addressee still receives mail at this address; with a check line for yes and a check line for no. The postal clerk will then check the appropriate line and you will have your answer. If the answer is no, you will have to continue sending forms to each new address you are provided with one that is current.

You may run into a postal clerk that tells you that under

no uncertain terms can you or will you be provided with the information that you are requesting. At that time you must ask to speak with the Postmaster. He or she is head honcho at the post office and every station has one. The Postmaster will be more familiar than a postal clerk with what can or can not be done legally. If you have a problem with the Postmaster simply get his or her information and write a letter stating what you are asking for and why. Supply your proof of a need for legal service and ask for assistance. After receiving your letter the Postmaster may then realize that you mean business and that you are not going away. If they are unfamiliar with the law most likely they will decide to take the time to find out the facts. A small suggestion that you may consider legal action for being denied your right to this information may cause them to think twice before they again turn you down. I do caution you to not make threats that you can't follow through. If you don't get anywhere with the post office you have other options available to you.

VOTER REGISTRATION RECORDS

If your obligor is civil minded, he or she might be a registered voter. If you move from the area where you initially registered to become a voter, you must re-register in the new area. Most registration offices require that you submit valid current identification when you register. If you have located a town or a city but can not find a street address for your obligor, this may be a good source for you. All voter registration information is open to the public and may also contain political party affiliation as well as a date of birth and occupation.

UTILITY COMPANY RECORDS

Utility Companies can be a good source of information. If your obligor skipped town but is still in the state somewhere this could be your gold mine. When most people move but stay within the same state they transfer their utility service to their new location. Utility companies are not supposed to give out this information but they do all the time. The best way to get information is to not be truthful about why you want it in the first place. I've always found it to be helpful to assume the identity of a more-than-helpful delivery person. It doesn't matter what company you pretend to be with; you can make one up if you want to. The important thing is that you play your part well. Your premise is that you are calling the utility company because John Doe ordered some merchandise from you that was on back order. The merchandise has just come in and you attempted to deliver it but the package was returned because he has moved and you do not know where he lives now. Could they please supply the current address so that you can re-deliver the merchandise? It's as simple as that. If the first customer service representative will not give you the address, hang up and call back. Keep calling until you get someone that will help you. If you get the same representative twice, hang up. You don't want them to flag the account for the next person to see. Refine and perfect your story with each call that you make. If being a delivery person is not your bag; you can be a nurse from John Doe's doctors office calling with test results and you urgently need to speak with him or her. Be creative; have fun with it. Sooner or later you will hit pay dirt.

DEPARTMENT OF MOTOR VEHICLE RECORDS

The department of Motor Vehicles in all states used to provide information the same way that the post office used to. But because of the Domestic Violence Act they too are curtailing whom they share information with. As of this writing there are several states that are prohibiting the release driver and registration record information. The exception to this rule is of course, if you are an attorney or a member of law enforcement.

Look up the number for the Motor Vehicle Department in your state in the phone book and call and ask them what their policy is. You may find that your state will still provide information as a matter of public record. In this case you will need to write a letter requesting the information, include the driver's full name, most recent address known, date of birth and social security number if you have it. There is a small fee involved as well, usually about $5.00. The Motor Vehicle Department will respond to you in writing with the requested information. Be sure to call both the departments of driver's records as well as the department of registration records. They are separate departments and may have different records on the obligor.

If someone at the Motor Vehicle Department says that they will not supply the information to you, send the letter anyway, who knows if the person you spoke with is up to date with policies? Also remember that if you have proof that you need a current address in order to serve legal documentation you will probably get more help than if you didn't.

Once you receive an address from Motor Vehicles be sure to verify it through the post office to be certain that it is current. If the obligor's driving record indicates that he or she has received tickets or has had accidents this may indicate the area where he or she spends a lot of time. Perhaps they live or work nearby...

NEIGHBORS

Former neighbors are another good resource of information. If the obligor is no longer living at the last address known to you use the City Directory to get telephone numbers of his or her former neighbors. The City Directory will provide you with the address and telephone number of the person that you are searching for as well as the same information for the people that live nearby. If the obligor lived in an apartment building you will find names, addresses and telephone numbers of other people that live in the same building. If he or she lived in a house you will find names, addresses and telephone numbers for the people that lived next door, down the block, across the street, etc. You could take this as far as you want to. Call them with the same delivery person technique. It works great with neighbors. You would be surprised at the amount of information an unsuspecting neighbor will regurgitate if you sound sincere enough. Good neighbors are always willing to help other good neighbors. If you find that your obligor was not a good neighbor at all, then you should be truthful about who you are and what you are trying to do. Your obligor's former neighbor will likely be pleased to help you catch your bandit. Pump them for whatever you can get.

FORMER LANDLORDS

The best former landlords to find will be the ones where the obligor skipped out owing rent. They will be happy to help, especially if you tell them that you will relay to them information on the whereabouts of the obligor once he or she is found. If your obligor left on good terms with the landlord then you may not be able to talk them into giving you private information on one of their former tenants. Subpoena any information that you might need from an unyielding former landlord. They may have details that the obligor listed on their rental application that will be helpful to you. If you are lucky enough to find the landlord before they refund a security deposit to the obligor you can garnish the refund. Chapter 10 covers garnishments.

FORMER EMPLOYERS

Former employers are similar to former landlords in that if the obligor was a horrible employee and caused nothing but problems, the employer may be willing to provide you with whatever information that will be helpful. If the obligor left on suitable terms you can forget about the employer being helpful to you at all, with the exception of the subpoena, of course.

CLIENTS

If the obligor is self-employed and you know whom some of his or her clients are, they too will be able to provide information on the whereabouts of the obligor. Certainly clients know how to get in contact with someone that is providing a service to them! Not only that but they will also be able to fill you in on how much money they supplied to the obligor over the past year – or more if they have an on-going relationship. If they were provided with references before they did business with the obligor the references will be able to help you as well. The biggest bonus though is the humiliation that the obligor will suffer when his or her client confronts them about the subpoena they've received from someone whom is trying to collect child support from him or her. Humiliation may be enough to cause the obligor to want to pay you so that it doesn't happen again. Whatever works is to your advantage.

CAREER LICENSES

What does the obligor do for a living? Is he or she a doctor, lawyer, Indian chief or anything else that requires a license? If so, check with the source of where they must be licensed and you may find current address information. Most licensing bureaus have detailed information that is available to the public. The address that you find may be a business address not a home address, but it's better than not finding anything at all and obligor's can be served at their business address. Is he or she a plumber, stock trader, trucker, or an insurance agent? They must all be licensed. Maybe the obligor works for a supermarket and belongs to a union. Trade unions should have information as well.

OBLIGORS IN THE MILITARY

Did your obligors join the military, get shipped off to some foreign country and you have no idea where he or she is? Collecting from military employees can be difficult so there is an entire chapter focused on just that. For our purposes in this chapter however, you should know that there are special military locators available through the government for a fee. Should you decide to take that route see Chapter17 on Collecting from Military Personnel for more information.

ALUMNI ASSOCIATIONS

Alumni associations keep current addresses on graduates for informational purposes. Dream up a good enough reason and they too will tell you whatever they know. The schools that the obligor attended may also have information so that they can send invitations to reunion parties.

HOBBIES

Does the obligor ride a bike? If so, has he or she ever had

a bike permit? If the answer is yes, they may have a permit in the town that they live in now. Has the obligor ever had a gun license, fishing or hunting license? These licenses are all a matter of public record in most areas. What hobbies does the obligor pursue?

FAMILY AND FRIENDS

Surely you must know some of the obligor's family and friends. Contact them for information. Start by trying to appeal to their to their conscience. Let them know that child support is something that your children need. They may have lead in their head and won't budge to help you one bit. Or they may want to help you but feel like they will be betraying their family member or friend if they do. You can rely on the subpoena in this case-it's like a magic wand. Wave it around in someone's face and poof, like magic you get what you want. Of course you will want to start your inquisitions with the family members or friends that the obligor has stiffed in some way. They will be the ones most likely to spill the beans.

OTHER GOVERNMENT RECORDS

If the obligor owns a business, they are registered with the state somewhere. Check Corporation records partnership and assumed business records with the Secretary of the State that the obligor lives in. This information can be given over the telephone. Does the business that the obligor operates collect any sales tax? If so, they must have a license and this information is available to the public. Other licenses to check: dog license, parking permit, sign permit, fire permit, vending permit...

REAL ESTATE TAX RECORDS

If the obligor owns any real property he or she will be listed with the county along with the property that they own, the amount of taxes that they pay, and the most current address known. This information is all public knowledge and can be obtained over the telephone.

CRIMINAL RECORDS

If the obligor has been in trouble with the law, the county where the offense occurred will have a lot of information on him or her. Contact the probation or parole officer, if there is one and get information from that source. The more recent the violation, the more recent the information that you receive will be. If the violation is an old one, it will only be useful to make contact if you are searching for a social security number or perhaps the name of family or friends. Any other information will most likely be outdated.

OTHER COURT RECORDS

Has the obligor recently divorced, or is he or she divorcing? Have they recently been sued or are they suing anyone? All of these matters are public records and any information that you can not get immediately, if anything at all, you can subpoena.

CREDIT REPORTS

Credit reports are one of the most valuable tools available to you. It is difficult to operate in today's society without some type of credit or without someone checking your credit worthiness for evaluation. Through a credit report you can get the most current address available, employment and asset information as well as details on the obligor's credit history and financial standing. In short, you can get everything you need to declare war. The one obstacle you have will be finding someone that will run a credit report on the obligor for you. As a judgement creditor you have a legal right to this information, but the credit bureaus will not give it to you. Unless you operate a company that extends credit to consumers or are an attorney you are plum out of luck. That is, of course, unless you have friends in high places that will get a copy of the report for you, or unless you hire someone to obtain one for you. If you don't mind waiting forever, using a government attorney through the state child support agency is the simplest way to get one since they are familiar with this practice and obtain reports on obligors frequently. If you do mind waiting forever contact several attorneys that specialize in collections until you find one that will be willing to run a report for you, for a fee, of course. If you have decided to hire an attorney, hopefully you have already found one that has this capability. Once you have the report call the credit bureau and ask them to help you interpret it.

LOCATOR SERVICES

The child support agencies also have two locator services available to them. One is a state locator service the other is a federal locator service. Custodial parents that are on AFDC can use these services without charge, all others are customarily charged a fee of approximately $10 with a maximum fee set at $25 although the state often absorbs all or most of the cost.

The state locator service is a computer network that will check all state records available in an effort to locate the obligor. If they are unsuccessful they will send the file to the federal service and they will conduct a search of federal records. If the federal locator is unable to locate the obligor through all the means available to the federal government they must by law, continue to search for the obligor every three months for three years.

Having the government to conduct the search for you through all of their means sounds like a great idea. But all that glitters is not gold. The state locator has 75 days to complete their search and report back to you with a hit or miss. If they forward the file for a federal service the time it takes to get back to you can vary. In the time it can take them to get back to you after all of their searches are done you and your children can starve to death. It is not uncommon for this process to take a year or longer. This is why you may need to take matters into your own hands at times.

When you visit your state agency to request a locator service, you will be asked to fill out a "registration of absent or puntative parents" and pay the fee requested. Ask them at that time to run the state and the federal locator service concurrently to save you some time and headache. It is a common practice to exhaust the resources of the state locator before running the federal, but it does not have to be done that way. You may be told that if you are not on welfare or if you are not receiving the services of the state agency that you can not apply for locator services, but that is untrue. Press on and insist that they check the guidelines. Anyone who requests this service is entitled to it as long as they pay the fee.

PRIVATE INVESTIGATORS

If you get fed up and are considering hiring a private investigator there are some guidelines that you should follow to insure that you don't get taken advantage of.

1. Decide how much money you are willing to spend and don't let the investigator talk you into spending any more. Include the investigator's expenses in this amount since they are not included in the fee quoted to you. You may decide that an investigator is too costly.

2. Get an agreement on what expenses you will be expected to pay for and get it in writing.

3. Get an agreement on what the hourly rates are and get it in writing.

4. Ask for an accounting of the investigator's time and expenses.

5. Ask how the investigation will be conducted. Fieldwork will be a lot less cost efficient than telephone work.

6. Put the entire agreement in writing.

7. Ask for at least three references that can recommend him or her based on his or her skip tracing abilities.

8. Agree on written progress reports and ask that you receive them frequently.

9. In your agreement be sure to have a clause where you can terminate the investigator at any time, with a full refund on any unused retainers, if you are not happy with the service.

10. If you do terminate your investigator do not have any further contact with him or her until you receive your refund. They may charge you for whatever

conversation they have with you and then tell you that you have no money left to refund.

SERVICE BY PUBLICATION

When all else fails and you are unable to locate the absent parent/obligor to serve him or her with legal papers, the law allows you to serve them by publication. This means that you must place an advertisement in the newspaper where the obligor is last known to have lived that he or she is being sued for child support. The advertisement must appear in the section where legal notices are posted and must include all of the pertinent information. This is a common practice and is allowable by law. You must get the judge's permission to serve the absent parent/obligor by publication. To do this you must file a motion with the court and ask the judge to sign it. Ask the clerk's office if they have pre-printed forms. If they do not, visit the office supply store nearest you and get one there. Item #4 is the motion that you need.

MOTION AND ORDER TO ALLOW
SERVICE BY PUBLICATION

IN THE CIRCUIT COURT OF THE STATE OF ANY STATE
FOR THE COUNTY OF ANY COUNTY

In the Matter of	)	
	)	No. 0000
JANE DOE,	)	
Petitioner	)	
	)	
and	)	
JOHN DOE	)	MOTION AND ORDER
Respondent	)	TO ALLOW SERVICE
	)	BY PUBLICATION

Jane Doe, petitioner in the above-captioned matter, hereby moves the Court for an order allowing Service by Publication.

This motion is based upon the attached affidavit, which is incorporated herein by reference.

_____
JANE DOE
Petitioner

ORDER

IT IS SO ORDERED.

DATED this _____ day of _____, 199__.

_____
CIRCUIT COURT JUDGE

ITEM #4: MOTION AND ORDER TO ALLOW SERVICE BY PUBLICATION

Chapter 9: Locating The Assets

If you have located the obligor the next step is to find his/her assets so that you can take them and cash them in. Using many of the same methods that you used to locate the obligor, you can locate his/her assets. The only difference is that the first time you were looking for a current address of the obligor so that you could serve him/her legal papers; now you are looking for their income or assets that you can convert into income. Contrary to popular belief, income is not only what a person earns. *"Unearned income"* is considered to be income as well. That is, income that is not earned through a paycheck. Examples may include rental incomes, dividends and interest from stock ownership, etc. Virtually everything that belongs to the obligor can be construed as income or converted into income for your usage. You just have to know where to look and what to look for.

CREDIT REPORTS
As you have found in Chapter 8, credit reports can reveal an enormous amount of information that can be helpful to you.

They can help you to locate an obligor that has skipped out on you. They can also help you find out what they own. If you do not have access to a credit reporting system, find someone that does and pay them to run a report on the obligor for you, as described in chapter 8.

This is what you will be looking for:

1. If you haven't done so already, confirm the home address that's listed on the credit report with the post office. Next, find out if the obligor owns the home that they live in. If they do, consider the option of placing a *judgement lien* on the property and threaten to force a foreclosure on the property unless you are paid in full. See Chapter 10.

2. Does the obligor own any other real estate? Again, consider the option of forcing a foreclosure on the property.

3. Does the obligor own cars, boats, motorcycles or anything else that's valuable? Consider the option of filing a writ of execution with the Court so that you can have the property seized and sold at an auction. See Chapter 10. Do a drive-by look-see of the house that the obligor lives in to see what you can find.

4. If the obligor does not own the property that he/she is living in, find out who the owner of the property is; you learned how to do this in Chapter 8. Subpoena the landlord to discover whether the obligor has a security deposit or not. If he/she does have a deposit, file a *writ of garnishment* to have the money released to you. See Chapter 10. A savvy landlord may decide to contest the garnishment contending that he/she is a lienholder on the account. Most people, including landlords, don't contest garnishments; they don't know that they can. If they do contest it, there is no guarantee that the judge will stop the garnishment from going through. If the judge will not stop the garnishment, the money is yours and the obligor will have to come up with another security deposit. If the judge does stop it, at the very least you can file a *judgement lien* against the deposit. When the obligor moves from the apartment that he/she is renting, the money will be refunded to you as long as he/she does not owe anything to the landlord at the time of the move. If he/she does move owing money and the deposit is refunded to the landlord; at least you tried. Better luck on the next attack.

5. If the credit report reveals a current employer, have the obligor's wages withheld and/or garnished if you haven't done so already. See chapter 10 for details.

6. When you contact the employer ask if the obligor receives any bonuses or commissions. Also ask if he or she has any company savings plans or deductions like an IRA or a 401K. Does he/she own any company stock? Does he/she have a pension plan? These items can all be considered income for the purposes of child support collection. If the obligor has any of these benefits, Chapter 10 will tell you how to tap into them for past due child support.

7. Subpoena the employer to send you a copy of the front and back of the last paycheck that the obligor cashed. The back of the paycheck may reveal the bank where the obligor has his/ her checking account and may also reveal his/her account number. Once you are in receipt of the banking information, you will be able to garnish the obligor's checking account for past due support money. Previous employers are good for this information as well.

8. While you are at it, subpoena the bank for other accounts that they may be holding for the obligor. Usually a savings account or CD's will be kept with the same bank that holds one's checking account. If you find other accounts they can be garnished as well.

9. If employers, or former employers, do not have any information to supply to you, try the trade union where the obligor belongs. Trade unions should be able to supply "earned income" information as well as information on any benefits, bonuses, commissions, and union benefits received by the obligor.

10. If the obligor is the owner of business that requires a license costing a lot of money to get – a liquor license, for example; file a judgement lien against it. Without a license, the restaurant or bar that the obligor operates cannot serve liquor and that can be damaging to a business of that sort. In a case like this, the license itself will most likely mean nothing to you. Most times they cannot be sold so you will not be able to convert it into money that way. However, if the obligor's business can go down the tubes without the license they may be inclined to pay you the past due child support to regain the usage of the license that now belongs to you. Who knows - you may be able to find a way to have the license legally sold after all. The worst case scenario would be that the obligor doesn't pay you one dime in past due child support and you don't relinquish the control over the liquor license. Your position hasn't changed any because you weren't getting any support anyway, but the obligor's business will be damaged in some way, if not completely. It's not a bad deal since you still have other tactics to use.

11. If you find any credit card accounts, loans, or any other means of credit listed on the obligor's credit report, subpoena the original application that the obligor completed from the creditor or lender. It may contain information on other assets that are not listed on the credit report. These may be assets that you can garnish or otherwise convert into income.

12. If you are able to locate a CD (Certificate of Deposit) owned by the obligor you could either garnish the interest that the CD earns or through a *writ of execution* you can have the deposit turned over to you. Figure out what will bring you the greatest return before you make your decision.

13. If you know the obligor to be a stockholder for publicly traded stock, you will need to subpoena information regarding his/her stock portfolio from the broker. It helps if you know who the broker is or the company they work for. If not, you will have to find out through one of your sleuthing techniques or go through a government attorney to have a *1099* search done. See chapter 10. The government attorney will be able to use federal records to access *1099* information (interest earned from banks or other financial institutions) of the obligor's. The attorney will be able to find out where the earned interest has come from and what company is holding the money. This information will then be reported back to you and you can then subpoena the broker for details on the stock that the obligor owns. A government attorney is the only person that can access *1099* information.

14. Chapter 10 tells you how to seize personal property

belonging to the obligor. This property can be sold and the profit applied to back child support. Follow the methods outlined when you find property on the credit report or through any of your other means.

15. If the obligor owns or at sometime owned an aircraft or boat, check to see if it is still registered in his/her name. If it is, you have hit the jackpot; move to seize and sell it immediately. Aircraft registrations are listed with both the Federal Aviation Administration, (call 405-954-3011), and with the state. A boat will be listed with the state, unless its size and tonnage (weight) stipulates that it be listed with the government as well. To find out, call the state Marine Board and the U.S. Coast Guard.

16. Those obligors that are in the military and other federal employees that may be difficult to collect from can have their income garnished. See the Chapters that focus exclusively on these matters.

17. If the obligor receives income from a trust fund, subpoena information about the fund, from the trustee. Once you know what income the obligor receives from the fund, you can either place a wage withholding on the income or have the income garnished.

18. If you believe that the obligor will be receiving an inheritance through someone's will, contact the government office that handles wills in the county where it will be eventually probated and ask for a copy. If he/she is listed as a beneficiary, have a lien placed on any money due to the obligor.

19. If an immediate family member of the obligor dies without a will, and you believe that the obligor may receive some inheritance, you may be able to place a lien on the obligor's share of the estate. For this you will need to contact an attorney.

20. A percentage of unemployment benefits can be withheld for child support payments. Subpoena information from the obligor's previous employer to find out when the obligor lost his/her job and any other details that may be important for you to know. Then contact the unemployment office to find out what information they need from you to begin withholding some of the benefits that the obligor receives. Some states will not allow an obligee or their private attorney to have unemployment benefits withheld. If the state that the obligor lives in will not allow you to withhold wages, you must work through the state child support agency. Government attorneys are given more leeway in this area and will be able to get a withholding in any state.

21. Workers compensation benefits can also be withheld for child support. If the obligor's employer will not tell you who their insurance carrier is; subpoena them for the information. Contact the carrier to request the address they are using to send checks to the obligor, the amount of the checks that they are sending, and when will the benefits run out. Of course you will need to ask what information you need to forward to them to get your process started.

22. If the obligor is disabled in some way, you and/or your child may be entitled to disability payments. Pay a visit to the Social Security Administration office in your area to find out. If you need to know whether the obligor is receiving Social Security benefits, you will have to go through a government attorney.

23. If the obligor has received, or is due to receive a settlement from a lawsuit, you can have this income garnished. Visit the county courthouse in the area where the suit was filed and obtain the names of the attorneys that are representing both the obligor and the person or entity that he/she is suing. File a writ of garnishment against the funds that the obligor is due to receive. If the state that the obligor lives in will not allow you to do this, although most of them will, keep close tabs on the lawsuit and file your garnishment immediately following the settlement. Do not let the obligor know what you are doing. If you do, he/she will probably try to hide the money as quickly as it comes in.

24. If you can not find any assets that belong to the obligor and you become really desperate, you can search the obligor's trash for anything that might lead to asset information. Look for credit card receipts, bank deposit slips, statements, etc. Once trash is put out on the curb it is public property so you won't be breaking any laws.

25. You can also become a phony survey person. Before

I got my job as a bill collector for the bank, I worked as a marketing research surveyor. I would call people at their homes to ask their opinions on a variety of topics. I have handled everything from political surveys, to surveys about the newest brand of peanut butter. At the end of every survey that I was able to get completed before the consumer hung up on me, I was instructed to ask some personal questions. These questions included what they did for a living, their address, where they banked, and then, of course, would you like to receive a coupon for a free jar of peanut butter (or whatever else it was that was the topic). The surveys that I was assigned to were almost always successful if the consumer knew that they were going to get something at the end. Search your mind for something that you think the obligor would like to have and that they would be willing to disclose certain information to get. Most people like free things. The danger is to be certain that you make the survey sound believable. Once you have an idea of your "offering", decide what information you need to get from the obligor. Your list might include: where do you bank, what is your occupation, are you married, do you hold MasterCard/visa accounts, what is your approximate income, etc. Then get to work and put together your "survey". It might go something like this:

Survey person:	Hello may I speak with Mr. John Doe?
Obligor:	This is John Doe
Survey person:	Mr. Doe, this is Mary Jackson from MMM Marketing in the Ohio Theatre Group and would like to give you four free front row center tickets to our next production of Les Miserables, just for answering a few questions.
Obligor:	Okay
Survey person:	When is the last time that you have been

to the theatre?

Obligor:	Oh, about 6 months ago
Survey person:	How often would you say that you attend the theatre?
Obligor:	About two or three times a year
Survey person:	When you purchase tickets for the theatre do you pay for them on a MasterCard or Visa account? By answering this question please know that we will not place you on a mailing list of any type.
Obligor:	I usually pay by MasterCard
Survey person:	And which bank is that under?
Obligor:	Peoples bank of North America
Survey person:	Do you bank with People's as well?
Obligor:	Yes
Survey person:	How many theatre shows have you seen in your lifetime?
Obligor:	I don't know, maybe fifteen
Survey person:	If you have children, do you take them to theatre shows?
Obligor:	No, I don't take them
Survey person:	Just a few more questions and then we are done. What is your approximate age?

Under 30 or over 30?

Obligor:	Over 30
Survey person:	What is your occupation?
Obligor:	I'm a licensed plumber
Survey person:	And your income – is it over or under $50,000?
Obligor:	Over $50,000
Survey person:	Thank you for your time Mr. Doe. You will receive a letter in the mail from the Ohio theatre Company within 14 days. The letter will include a number for you to call to claim your free tickets and reserve seats for the show. Have a great day!
Obligor:	Thank you

Of course you will want to customize your letter to the obligor with a survey that makes sense to you. It's better if you ask someone else to make the call for you so that there's no chance that the obligor will recognize your voice. Also, be sure not to use the names of companies that actually exist. Use your imagination and create names that sound real. The obligor will never know the difference. The key is in the presentation. Sound confident and sincere.

Chapter 10: Enforcement Steps You Can Take

Statistics reveal that only 25% of the custodial parents that have child support orders ever receive their money. Therefore, 75% of the child support orders that are written aren't worth the paper they are printed on. Having a child support order means nothing, unless you get paid. Let's recount what you have learned so far: You have learned how to establish paternity and what to do if you are underage. You have learned how to get a child support order and how to have your order modified if your circumstances have changed. You can find your deadbeat if he/she skips town and you are able to effectively hire a private attorney and maybe even get legal services for free. You now also know what is legally considered to be income – it's not just what one gets in their paycheck. Now, one way or the other, you will learn the steps that you can take yourself to get blood from an unyielding stone. Ready? One, two, three, SQUEEZE!

If truth can be told, there are many options that you have to get your money. The problem is that most people don't know about them. The officials that are paid to help you either don't know about them or they don't want to tell you about them because most likely it will give them more work. By now you have noticed that this book is about work. How much work are you willing to do to collect your money? Just how mad are you? Are you not going to take it anymore? If you are willing to do the work, then you will get your money.

Most people know about wage withholding. That's when they take the money that due to you directly from the obligors paycheck. But that's not all there is. That's only the beginning and we will begin there because it is the simplest way to get what you want.

WAGE WITHHOLDING:

A wage withholding (also called an order withholding earnings or a payroll deduction) is a court order requiring the obligors' employer to deduct money from his/her paycheck and forward it to you or to the state agency. It is the easiest way to collect your money and it has a lot of benefits. 1. Once notified and presented with a court order the employer can not refuse to deduct and forward the money. 2. The money must be forwarded within 10 days of the deduction. 3. If the obligor quits or is fired, the employer is required to inform you. They are also required to tell you where the new job is if they know. 4. Under federal law, a wage withholding must be permitted for anyone that has a child support order where the payments are 30 days past due or if three consecutive payments have been missed. So as long as the obligor keeps their job, you will have a steady payment coming to you. Keep in mind that typically you can only get about 60% of the paycheck amount plus an additional 5% for arrearages over twelve weeks if the obligor has not re-married and has no dependents. If the obligor has re-married and has dependents, the amount that can be deducted decreases to 50% and 5% for arrearages over twelve weeks. You can get a wage withholding through your local child support agency or by going to court yourself and filing an order to withhold earnings. Take a look at Item #5. It is the document that says *exparte* order to withhold earnings. This is the motion you will use when you file for wage withholding so take a few moments to familiarize yourself with it.

Simply get the form from a supply store, fill it out and submit to the court clerk. The small fee involved will probably be about $5.00.

WAGE GARNISHMENT:

Many people confuse wage withholdings with wage garnishments. They use the two terms interchangeably as though they mean the same thing. Be aware: they don't have the same meaning nor do they work the same way. While a wage withholding is an order from the court to deduct a certain amount of money on a continuous basis and send it to you regularly; a wage garnishment (item #6) is an order from the court to deduct one lump sum of money (usually a large sum) and send it to you. A wage garnishment is a one-time deal. You will not get regular payments and it does not permit for future child support that may become due. It does have its benefits though. How would you like to go to court for past due child support, get awarded a judgement for the amount past due, and then have that entire amount taken out of the obligors check at once! It can be done. Just thinking of it gives me goose pimples.   Remember that the only way you could lose your court case is if the money is not owed to you. If you have a court order in place, and the obligor is in the arrears, the only defense he/she has is mistaken identity. If he/she does not show up in court, you automatically win.

INTERSTATE WAGE WITHHOLDING:

If your obligor lives in another state you can still get a wage withholding. Simply visit the child support office in your area and they will handle the whole thing for you. If you are pursing the case on your own it's not much different than handling a case that's in state. Prepare the forms and bring them to the family court in your county and give them to the clerk. You will then have to arrange to have the order served to the employer. If you have an obligor on your hands that is a real pain in the neck, prepare yourself to bulldoze him/her. This goes for the interstate

EX PARTE ORDER TO WITHHOLD EARNINGS

IN THE CIRCUIT COURT OF THE STATE OF ANY STATE
FOR THE COUNTY OF ANY COUNTY

JANE DOE,   )   No. 0000
     Petitioner,   )

)
     and   )   EX PARTE ORDER
)   TO WITHHOLD EARNINGS

JOHN DOE,   )
     Respondent   )
TO: Employer   John Doe
        Address   Social Security Number

Based upon Petitioner's Motion,
YOU ARE   DELINQUIENT
HEREBY   AMOUNT OWED $_____
ORDERED TO   CONTINUING MONTHLY
WITHHOLD &   SUPPORT
PAY OVER TO: PAYMENTS: $ _____

     An amount equal to 25 percent (or the continuing monthly support payment amount, whichever is less) of the beneficiary's benefits for temporary total disability, or an amount equal to 25 percent of the beneficiary's benefits for permanent partial disability and permanent total disability due or becoming due for each month beneficiary becomes or is eligible for these benefits, whether the benefits are paid monthly or in a lump sum payment.
     The Department of Human Resources will inform you when there is no longer a current monthly support obligation.

     EVEN IF THERE IS MORE THAN ONE ORDER TO WITHHOLD, IN NO EVENT SHALL YOU WITHHOLD MORE THAN 25 PERCENT OF BENEFICIARY'S BENEFITS DUE OR BECOMING DUE FOR EACH MONTH BENEFICIARY BECOMES OR IS ELIGIBLE.
     THIS ORDER supercedes any order to withhold previously entered and shall continue in effect as long as there is current support owed or until further order of this court.

DATED _____   _____
                             CIRCUIT COURT JUDGE

ITEM #5: EX PARTE ORDER TO WITHHOLD EARNINGS

Writ of Garnishment

IN THE _____ COURT OF THE STATE OF ANY STATE

For the county of _____.

_____.

_____Plaintiff   Case No. _____
                                       Writ of Garnishment

_____

_____ Defendant(s)

IN THE NAME OF THE STATE OF ANY STATE, TO: _____

    You are now a garnishee

    AS A GARNISHEE, YOU NEED TO KNOW THE FOLLOWING (the following information is to be filled in by the creditor):

    On _____, 19__, plaintiff/defendant(cross out one)_____, Named above and called "Creditor", has obtained a judgement (a court order for the payment of money) against the plaintiff/defendant (cross out one) _____, named above and called "Debtor". The Debtor's social security number or employee identification number is _____ (insert if known).
The following amount is necessary to satisfy the Creditor's judgement:

+Judgement debt	$_____	_____	$ _____
+Prejudgement interest	$_____	_____	$ _____
+Attorney Fees	$_____	Total other from additional sheet	
+Cost Bill	$ _____	(if used)	$ _____
+Post-Judgement Interest	$ _____	+ Past Writ Issuance Fees	$ _____
+Delivery Fee for this Writ	$ _____	+ Past Delivery Fees	$ _____
+Sheriff Fees other than		+ Transcript and Filing Fees	
Delivery Fees	$ _____	for other counties	$ _____
+Other (Explain. Attach additional		= Subtotal	$ _____
sheets if necessary.)	$ _____	LESS Payments Made	($ _____)
_____	$ _____	= TOTAL Amounts Required to Satisfy	
_____	$ _____	in Full this Judgement	$ _____

THE CLERK OF THE COURT HAS NOT CALCULATED ANY AMOUNTS ON THE WRIT AND IS NOT LIABLE FOR ERRORS MADE IN THE WRIT BY THE CREDITOR.

I certify that I have read the Writ of Garnishment; and to the best of my knowledge, information and belief, there is good ground to support it.
    DATED _____, 19 ____

        Signature of Creditor's Attorney_____
        Type or Print Creditor's Attorney _____
        Address _____Date ____

ITEM #6: WRIT OF GARNISHMENT

obligors as well as the obligor that live in state. Reread chapter 9 and withhold earnings or garnish anything and everything that the obligor receives as income. We are not just talking about paychecks here. The plan is to make his/ her life so miserable that they would rather pay you than to constantly have their funds intercepted.

WRIT OF GARNISHMENT (PERSONAL PROPERTY):

Paychecks are not the only things that can be garnished. Any liquid property (cash) that the obligor owns can be garnished for child support. This includes savings and checking accounts, CD's, stock, etc. Personal property that is not money, but that can be seized and sold for money, can also be garnished. In the event that you have found the obligors liquid assets (cash) and you would like to seize them (take them away) you will need to file a writ of garnishment. A writ of garnishment is filed with a banking institution, employer or some other third party that is holding money for the obligor. This is different from a wage garnishment because a wage garnishment takes money directly and only from earnings. A writ of garnishment takes money from a source where the money is just sitting. Some examples might be bank accounts, IRAs, etc. If your obligor has taken their liquid property (cash) from whatever source and transferred it to a friend or relative to prevent you from getting your hands on it, you must obtain it in another way. In this instance you must file what is called a *creditor's bill*. We will discuss creditor's bills later.

A writ of garnishment is an order from the court demanding that the third party that is holding money for the obligor turn it over to the court. Similar to the wage garnishment, it is a one-time lump sum that does not provide for future child support, but it can pay you what's past due. If you have a child support order and the obligor owes you $3000.00 in past due support and you find an account with $3500.00 in it, you can have the account "garnished" for $3000.00. If the account you find has only $800.00, you can wipe out the $800.00 and the obligor will still owe the remaining $2200.00.

When you have located the funds in the bank or other

banking institution, call them and ask what their specific procedures are. Most institutions have several branches and you will need to know which branch needs to be served with your writ. Then go to your office supply store and get a bank garnishment form. Complete the form and take it to the court clerk with whatever small fee they require and file the paperwork. You will also need to arrange to have the paperwork served. See item # 5 – writ of garnishment.

Writs must be answered in five days. Generally, you will not have a problem with a banking institution since they are accustomed to receiving documents of this type. Once the court receives the money they are required to hold it for approximately 10 days before they release it to you. This gives anyone who denies owing the money a chance to request a hearing. Common objections are that the money belongs to someone other than the obligor or that the money is exempt from garnishment.

If the obligor states that the money belongs to someone other than him or herself, they must be able to prove this. If they say that a portion of the funds are exempt, and can prove it, you will receive the remaining balance. An example of exemption would be: In most states you are only permitted to take a percentage of the obligor's paycheck during a garnishment - usually 25%. If the obligor can prove that the entire $3,000.00 that was taken from his bank account consisted of deposited paychecks, then you would be entitled to 25% of each paycheck. If the obligor deposited 3 weekly paychecks, of $1,000.00 a week, you would get $750.00 and the rest would be returned. In the meantime, however, you would have certainly ticked him/her off and maybe shook them up enough to decide to pay up and not to mess with your child support anymore. In addition, if this were a checking account that the money was taken from, checks would be bouncing all over town. If the money was obtained from a CD or stock that had to be sold, the interest would be lost and perhaps there would be penalties to pay. Now, doesn't that make you smile?

WRIT OF EXECUTION (PERSONAL PROPERTY):

Personal property that is in the hands of the obligor can also be taken away. It can then be sold and the profit turned over to you. This process is a bit more complicated and will cost you more to do, but the benefits can be great! Close your eyes for a moment and imagine the obligor leaving his or her workplace at the end of the day only to find that his car is gone. Better yet, he awakens early on a Saturday morning to a knock at the door. He opens the door and sees the sheriff standing there with an order in his hands to seize his household belongings. It can happen. But don't get your hopes up yet, the procedures that you must follow are enough to cause anyone to turn and walk away. So I ask you – how badly do you want your money?

A writ of execution first begins at your family clerk court office. There you will ask the clerk to file a writ of execution, which will cost you about $5.00. Item # 7 is a writ of execution. You will see that it instructs the sheriff to seize the property. The writ of execution must issued to the sheriff along with item # 8 which is a sheriff's instruction. A sheriff's instruction tells the sheriff what items must be seized. You must provide the sheriff with specific details of the item or the items on the list. If you are seizing a car for example, you must include the year, make, model, color, vehicle identification number, and some type of proof that the car belongs to the obligor. You must also tell the sheriff where the property will be located and when it will be there. The sheriff will charge you a fee for seizing the property; you can expect to pay about $50.00. You will also be required to post a bond in the event that the sheriff is sued for seizing property that should not have been taken. The amount of the bond will be based on the value of the property that is being seized. The sheriff may ask you to approximate the value of the property. If you are seizing a car, or any other personal property, and you estimate the value to be $10,000., you can expect to pay anywhere from $100 to $300 for the bond. As a rule of thumb, the bond will cost between 1% and 3% of the total estimated value of the property. You can get a bond by contacting a bondsman, insurance agent, or attorney. You will also be required to pay for a tow truck or a moving van for the items being removed. The sheriff will take the seized personal belongings to a storage facility, where they will stay, until the sheriff holds a "sheriff's sale" and the items are sold. You must also pay the storage fee. All of these fees must be paid up front before any seizure of personal property can take place. This is why you must be committed to "by any means necessary" policy to get your child support. You can see why many people do not go this route. Sure, you can add the fees that you had to pay out onto the judgement that the obligor owes to you, but if you are like most custodial parents, you don't have the money to put out. If the personal property that you wish to seize is worth a lot of money ... much more than would be required to satisfy your judgement and the additional fees entailed, including the cost of the sale, then you may consider enlisting help from someone in the form of a temporary loan. Keep in mind that you can only get the amount of money that the property sells for, minus the cost of the sale. If the car valued at $10,000 sells for $4,000 at the auction and the cost of the sale was $200, you will receive $3,800. If you invested $1,000 to have the property seized, you net $2,800.

So before you decide to seize personal property and have it sold to pay your past due child support, check your numbers and make sure that you don't get caught behind the eight ball.

There are also some items that the government will not permit you to take from the obligor, because they may be essential to his/her basic living. These items are exempt. A car or any furniture is exempt up to the value of $1,500. Books and tools are exempt up to $750, and a rifle up to $500. So the car in the above example would be exempt up to a value of $1,500. Instead of receiving $3,800 as stated above, because of the automatic $1,500 exemption, you would receive $2,300. Once you deduct your investment of $1,000, your net is $1,300. Food for thought: you could always have the personal property seized and sold and willingly break even just for the fun of it.

You could also bid on the property yourself, up to the amount of your judgement and walk away with it without any out of pocket costs. Pay a little extra, if you like, just to own the

WRIT OF EXECUTION

In the _____ court of the State of Any State

For the County of _____

_____   No. _____

_____.

Plaintiff

    Vs.   **EXECUTION**

_____.

_____.

Defendant

To _____ County, Any State

WHEREAS ON _____ in the _____ Court of _____County, Any State, _____
Recovered a judgement from _____
_____ for the following sum(s):

Which judgement, or a certified transcript thereof, was on _____, 19 _____, duly docketed in the judgement docket of the _____ Court of _____ County, Any State, where it remains in force and unsatisfied in whole or in part;

THEREFORE, IN THE NAME OF THE STATE OF ANY STATE, you are commanded that out of the personal property of the said judgement debtor(s), or if sufficient personal property cannot be found, then out of the real property belonging to said judgement debtor(s) on or after the date said judgement was docketed in your county, excepting such as the law exempts, that you satisfy the amount of said judgement with interest and costs and disbursments that may have accured, LESS the amount of $_____ which has been paid on said judgement, and also the costs of this writ, and make due return of this writ within sixty days after you receive this writ.

Witness my hand and the seal of this court on this _____ day of _____, 19_____

Judgement Debt	$_____	_____
Interest	$_____	Name and Title
Attorney Fee	$_____	
Cost Bill	$_____	By _____ Deputy
Additional Costs	$_____	
Total	$_____	
Payments Made	$_____	Issued at the request of:
Balance Dus	$_____	
Accruing Costs	$_____	
Disbursements	$_____	_____
Keeper's Fees	$_____	_____
Mileage	$_____	_____
Total	$_____	_____

ITEM #7: WRIT OF EXECUTION

SHERIFF'S INSTRUCTION

IN THE CIRCUIT COURT O FTHE STATE OF ANY STATE
FOR THE COUNTY OF ANY COUNTY

In the matter of:	)	
JANE DOE,	)	No. 1111
	)	
Petitioner	)	
	)	INSTRUCTIONS TO
and	)	SHERIFF
	)	
	)	(Any County)
JOHN DOE,	)	
	)	
Respondent	)	

TO THE SHERIFF OF ANY COUNTY:

      YOU ARE HEREBY INSTRUCTED to execute the enclosed Writ of Execution for the following described personal property of the defendant, to-wit:

      1990 BMW 550SL, New Jersey License Plate No. 115-GTW, VIN No. 569875699P

by immediately proceeding to debtor's residence located at 9 Any Street, Any Town, Any State Any Zip Code, or to such other location as may be hereafter identified within your county and at such place or places to then and there take possession of the equipment described above from the respondent or his agents or employees or any other person who may be in possession thereof and deliver it to the petitioner.

      Enclosed is our check in the amount of $50.00 as a deposit to cover your fees and expenses. If you have any questions or problems, please contact the undersigned. Thank you for your assistance.

                                     Your name or your attorney's name
                                     Street address
                                     Town, State, Zip Code
                                     Telephone Number with Area Code

ITEM #8: SHERIFF'S INSTRUCTIONS

property yourself. You can do this because you have a judgement for the amount of your unpaid child support, and you have a lien on the property. It is called a judgement lien. You can then sell it privately for more money if it is worth it. Or if it is a car that you seized, you can drive it around the obligor's neighborhood a few times. That's fun too.

WRIT OF GARNISHMENT (PERSONAL PROPERTY IN THE HANDS OF A THIRD PARTY):

Personal property that is in the hands of a third party can be garnished as well. The only drawback for you is that most people don't understand it. Banks are used to getting garnishments that they must fulfill, the neighborhood mechanic is not. For example: the fancy car that you want to garnish is at the dealership for it's scheduled and predictable 40,000 mile check up. You have the writ of garnishment served to the dealership and they have no choice but to hand the car over. In this instance they would have to contact the sheriff's department and let them know that the car is in their possession. The sheriff would come and remove the vehicle and place it in storage in the same manner as if it was taken from the obligor's home. The same procedures would then follow.

WRIT OF EXECUTION (REAL PROPERTY):

Writs of execution can also be filed against real property (real estate) to prevent someone from selling their property without paying you first, or to force a foreclosure in order to get your past due child support. They work similarly, but a writ of execution against real property is more complex. In this circumstance, it is best that you seek help from an attorney, if you can. Before you do, use your investigative techniques learned in chapter eight to discover the value of the house and how much equity the obligor has in it. Equity is the amount of money that has been invested into the property. For example, if a house was purchased for $100,000 and $50,000 has been put into the house between the down payment and mortgage payments, there is $50,000 of equity in the house. Since you will need to pay out a lot of fees to force the sale, and there are costs associated with the sale, you will need to know how much you can get out of the house before you proceed. Again, you need to keep yourself from getting behind the eight ball. The amount of money that is exempt will be between $12,000 and $15,000. Also confirm that their name is listed on the deed because you will need to prove that the house belongs to the obligor. In some states a home can not be foreclosed on at all because of the Homestead Act. Your trusty attorney should be able to tell you if your obligor is in one of those states.

Sounds like a headache, doesn't it? There is good news, however. When threatened with a foreclosure due to a judgement on their property, most people will find a way to pay the judgement rather than take the chance of losing their property. It's a game of "uncle". Sometimes just showing them that you mean business will get you what you want.

CREDITOR'S BILL

There are a countless number of cases where the obligor will go to any means to avoid paying child support. They will lie about their assets and income. They will place assets into a corporate name to avoid ownership. They have also been known to transfer assets into someone else's name, usually a new spouse or significant other. In this case you will need to file a motion that is called a creditor's bill. A creditor's bill is simply a lawsuit that you are filing against the person who is holding the property in question to prove that is was transferred to avoid paying you. This type of transfer of ownership is illegal. Once you are able to prove that the property used to belong to the obligor and that there is not a valid reason behind it, you will be able to get a judgement lien on the property and proceed with and a sheriff seizure or foreclosure. Again, check your numbers to make sure that it's worth it. One word of caution: this is another one of those complicated cases where you may need to enlist the help of an (ugh) attorney. At least you know what you need, and you know what to ask for.

TILL-TAP

This is one of my personal favorites. If your obligor owns a store that is open to the public and that has a cash register, wait until the busiest time of year and file a sheriff's instruction for a till-tap. During a till-tap the sheriff will go to the obligor's place of business and empty out the cash register - lock, stock, and barrel. Since you will want to get all the cash that you possibly can, you will want to instruct the sheriff to go after the busiest time of day. Hopefully there will still be some customers in the store to witness this action. If you don't know when is the busiest time of the year or of the day, do some research and find out. Call stores similar to the one that your obligor owns and tell them that you are doing some research, most people would be happy to answer a few short questions. Better yet, have someone that your obligor doesn't know to call his or her store and get the exact information that you need.

CREDIT REPORT INVESTIGATIONS

I know an obligor that left his wife and children and soon thereafter took up with another woman. He paid no child support to his family, though he was very wealthy. For five years, his first wife tried to track him down as he moved from state to state to avoid paying her. He placed money in over seas accounts and property in his new wife's name. They later adopted children and moved into a mansion. Because she was relentless, she eventually caught up with him and he was jailed. There are obligors that will fight tooth and nail to avoid paying child support. This man was obviously one of them. What disturbs me is that state agencies aided him and his new wife with the lifestyle that they led. If child support arrearages were noted on this man's credit report, he never would have been able to adopt the children that he and his wife had. This is one of the reasons that I am a staunch supporter of reporting past due child support to the credit agencies. It happens frequently. Obligors go on to live lavish lifestyles while leaving their children in the lurch. They purchase homes, new cars, take vacations and adopt children. If past due support was listed on credit reports they would not be able to accomplish such feats until the support was paid. Simply contact your local agency and insist that they do this. If your obligor owes you six months or more of past due child support, this is a federal law that you can use.

PAYMENT GUARANTEE

In some states, the court may require that the obligor post a bond, or a cash payment, to assure future child support. If the obligor fails to make a scheduled payment, the payment is taken from the bond, or cash payment, and forwarded to the custodial parent. In New York, when you file your court documents requesting a hearing for this matter, Cite 471 Family Court Act. In North Carolina, you must show that the obligor showed "intentional disregard for the financial obligation to the family". In other words, you must show that the obligor spent inordinate amounts of money on unnecessary goods. Instead of a bond or a cash payment, it is called a trust fund and it is set up for a period of three years.

If your state does not have a provision for the guarantee of payment, a letter to your Congressperson is in order. Write asking that she or he sponsor an Act for the guarantee of child support. Example:

If your Congressperson gets enough of these letters it would be nearly impossible for her or him to turn a deaf ear to the requests.

Date
Your name
Your street address
City, State, Zip Code

Congressperson Bill Brown
Street address
City, State, Zip Code

Dear Mr./Ms. Congressperson,

I am writing to request that you sponsor an Act for the guarantee of child support in (your state). New York and North Carolina have such laws. If the obligor repeatedly misses child support payments they may be required to post a surety bond or advance cash payment to provide for future child support payments in the event that they fall behind. If (your state) had such a law, it would aid in preventing my child support from lagging so far behind.

Please respond to this letter.

Sincerely,

Your name

Chapter 11: What The Courts Can Do For You

As you are working to get your child support, you will find that there are many people who will not be helpful to you. It may happen for a variety of reasons; sometimes it will simply be because they are ignorant and don't know how to help you. They may not know how to obtain the information that you are requesting to give it to you. It's easier to be rude to you, than to admit that they don't have the slightest idea of what you are asking. Depending on what source you go to and to whom you speak, they may be actively trying to protect the absent parent. And sometimes, it will be a combination of ineptitude and sheer meanness. Whatever the case, you don't have to feel as though you must beg for the information that you seek. If you have a legal and valid reason for digging into the personal financial life of someone, the law allows you to do it.

SUBPOENA

(Pronounced, suh-pee-nuh)

Let's say that you are certain that the obligor has accounts with an investment company, but you don't have any account numbers or any other means of proof. You call and/or write to the company and ask that they release the information to you on the basis that you have a judgement against their client. Not surprisingly, they refuse any information to you. If this happens to you, take comfort in the fact that you can subpoena any information that you wish to know from them (see item #9). You can find out how many accounts the obligor has, how much money are in them, when they were opened, as well as any personal information that they may have on the obligor. They may have a current address, employment information, other bank account or credit information – and it is all available to you through a subpoena. A subpoena is a court order that demands that the entity being subpoenaed (the investment company, in this case) appear as a witness to answer questions. In this case you would want to ask questions about the obligors finances and other personal information that they may have. If you want them to bring supporting documentation (statements, deposit slips, etc.), you must file a subpoena "duces tecum". This requires that they not only appear, but that they bring whatever paperwork you want them to bring. In most cases, you will only need to file subpoenas as a scare tactic. Once served with a subpoena, the most uncooperative person will suddenly provide you with what you need rather than take the time to appear and answer your questions. Simply contact them after they have been properly served and ask if they would prefer to provide the information that you request or if they would rather appear in person. Nine times out of ten, they will comply if it will get them off the hook. Remember to have them send to you copies of all of the supporting documents. Use the subpoena liberally. It can provide a wealth of information. If your obligor has moved out of town, without leaving a trace, and you are certain that someone in his/or her family must know where they are, though no one will say a word, you can subpoena them all to give you whatever information you need. A subpoena is issued under penalty of law, so they must comply or face the judge themselves. It's also a good way to get information from someone who would like to spill the beans but fears some type of

SUBPOENA

IN THE CIRCUIT COURT OF THE STATE OF ANY STATE
FOR THE COUNTY OF ANY COUNTY

JANE DOE,	)	
Plaintiff	)	No. 0000
	)	
vs.	)	CIVIL SUBPOENA
	)	DUCES TECUM
JOHN DOE,	)	
Defendant	)	

TO: Your obligor
          1515 Deadbeat lane
          Deadbeat City, NJ

IN THE NAME OF THE STATE OF ANY STATE:

You are hereby required to appear on the 1st day of August, 1996, commencing at 10:00 a.m., at the home of Jane Doe, Plaintiff, 430 You Owe Me Money Place, for your deposition by the plaintiff. You are required to appear and remain in attendance until the completion of your deposition. You are further required to bring with you any and all documents which are set forth on Exhibit A attached hereto and by reference incorporated herein.

      ISSUED this _____ day of _____, 1996.

ITEM #9: SUBPEONA

backlash. If they were subpoenaed, they would have no other choice but to talk. A subpoena can be a beautiful thing. Reread chapter 9 and consider the possibilities.

If the court clerk does not have a subpoena form you can get one from your local office supply store. After filling out the form it must be taken to the clerk's office to be signed and you must pay a small fee for this service (approximately $5.00). You must then have someone other than yourself, who is over the age of eighteen, to serve (deliver) the subpoena upon your witness. The only catch is that it must be personally delivered. It cannot be mailed or given to a secretary, co-worker, neighbor, etc. In addition, you must pay the witness for attending court and allow them mileage for the travel involved. You can expect to pay no more than $25.00 for an appearance and 10 cents per mile for travel. After the clerk signs the subpoena, you will need to make two copies of it. Keep one of the copies for yourself. The other copy and the original will need to be given to your "process server" (the person you select to serve the subpoena) to serve to your witness along with the fees for the appearance and mileage. Keep in mind that a witness may only be legally required to make an appearance to answer your subpoena if it is in the same county that they live in, work in, or conduct business in. Most people would be hesitant to snub a subpoena. If you can't get to the county that they live or work in, have it served anyway. They may not know that they don't have to appear.

If your witness would rather end up in a legal proceeding than to deal with you directly, you will need to provide a place for the *deposition* to take place. A *deposition* is the legal term for the question and answer period that will take place between you and your witness. A deposition can take place at almost any location. It does not have to be at a court building. If you do wish to have it at the courthouse you will have to arrange with the clerk to have a private room. Otherwise, it can take place at your home, office, the witness' home or office or anywhere else you desire. You will need to provide a court reporter. A court reporter is someone who will record the questions and answers during the deposition. Expect to pay $30 to $55 an hour for a

Court Reporter. You can get a *transcript* (written record) of the deposition for an additional fee. Be sure to ask what the fee is before you request one. By the end of your deposition you will have all the information that your witness can provide to you.

JUDGEMENT DEBTOR EXAM

Sometimes the only person that can provide the information that you need is the obligor himself/herself. If that is the case you will need to file a Judgement Debtor Exam. A Judgement Debtor Exam is similar to a subpoena in that the court is requiring someone to appear and answer questions. The difference between the two is that the subpoena is served upon any person, other than the obligor, who you would like to call as a witness, to come and answer questions about the obligor. A Judgement Debtor Exam is served upon the obligor to answer questions about his/her personal financials or whatever else may be necessary. The most difficult task when planning a Judgement Debtor Exam can be finding the obligor in order to have him or her served. In some cases you know where they are, you suspect or know that they have cash or assets, you just can't get to them. If you don't know where the obligor is, or if they tend to be a bit elusive and only come out at night like a vampire, then it makes your job more difficult. If your obligor is vampire-like, then you will need to re-read chapter 8 and find more methods to flush them out of the sewer. If you know where they are and they are doing a good job of hiding what they have, read on.

The first thing you should know is that rarely will a judge allow you to conduct a debtor exam until you have first attempted to execute on personal or real property, and failed, or until you have sent a demand letter (item#10) and it has been ignored. My personal strategy would be to send the demand letter first. Most deadbeats ignore demand letters, especially when they are from someone that they owe child support to. They will laugh it off and muse at the humor of it all. That's exactly what you want them to do. Of course you want your money and if after receiving your "Notice of Demand to Pay Judgement" your obligor pays you then you have what you want, right? Right. But what you don't have is the abundance of knowledge that a Judgement Debtor Exam can provide to you. During a debtor exam you can ask the obligor about cash he/she may have on hand, in an account, or invested. You may ask if anyone is holding any cash for him/her in any form. You may ask about any personal or real property that they may own or have transferred recently. In short you can find out the value of everything that they have. This serves two purposes for you: first, you can begin to form a list of things that you may want to have seized by the sheriff. If you have never been inside of the obligor's home how else would you know what they have? Second, it will do your soul good to have the deadbeat squirm a bit.

The obligor may lie during the exam, which is why you want to have him/her to bring all of their supporting documents so that you may examine them. This includes, but is not limited to tax returns, pay stubs, check books, bank statements, etc. You can make the list as long as you like as long as it is relevant. The obligor can also decide not to show up at the exam. If he/she decides not to show, the judge can order (and you will ask that the judge order) a bench warrant for his/her arrest. If your judge is a stick in the mud and will not order a warrant, he/she will order that a "show cause" hearing for contempt be held. This gives the obligor one last chance to appear and answer your questions. If he/she does not show a second time, a warrant will be issued. When the obligor is subsequently arrested, they will be held until you can get there to conduct your examination, or until they are able to post bail – if the judge sets a bail. The bail amount should be equal to the amount of past due child support. If the obligor is able to post bail, you can garnish it.

If the obligor lives in another state, or it would be too difficult for you to travel to conduct a judgement debtor exam, some states will allow you to do it by mail. This is called a *written interrogatory.* If you are interested in this method, call the clerk of the court in your county and ask if your state allows this type of debtor exam. You will be able to write down the list of questions that you want your obligor to answer. This list can be either personally delivered to the obligor or delivered by certified mail.

NOTICE OF DEMAND TO PAY JUDGEMENT

IN THE CIRCUIT COURT OF THE STATE OF ANY STATE
FOR THE COUNTY OF ANY COUNTY

JANE DOE,	)	NO. 0000
Plaintiff	)	
	)	
vs.	)	NOTICE OF DEMAND TO
	)	PAY JUDGEMENT
JOHN DOE,	)	
Defendant	)	

TO: John Doe
55 Deadbeat Lane
You Owe Me Money City, NJ   55555
Defendant.

DEMAND IS HEREBY MADE upon you pursuant to New Jersey Statutes, for payment, within ten days of your receipt of this Notice, of that certain Judgement entered against you in the above court.
Payment may be made through the court or to the undersigned.

PLEASE TAKE NOTICE THAT your failure to pay will result in further court proceedings. **TOTAL AMOUNT DUE: $5500.00.**
DATED this 1st day of August, 1996.

_____
Plaintiff

ITEM #10: NOTICE OF DEMAND TO PAY JUDGEMENT

The completed interrogatory must be returned to you within 20 days, along with any supporting documentation that you request. If it is not, the same procedure as above applies. Remember that each motion that you file will require small fees to be paid at the courthouse, as well as service fees if you hire a process server or the sheriff to serve the obligor. Only plan on conducting a debtor exam or interrogatory if you are dealing with high stakes and would bet your bottom dollar that the obligor is sitting on a gold mine that should belong to you and your children.

To conduct a "Judgement Debtor Exam," not only must you serve the obligor, but you must also file a motion with the court to conduct the exam (item#11). The motion must state where, when, and what time the obligor must appear in court. (The court clerk will provide you with this information when the judge signs your order – item #12). It must advise the obligor that he/she must answer questions under oath and, if you so desire, it may also provide a restraining order. The restraining order will advise the obligor that he/she may not sell, transfer or dispose of any assets before the exam takes place. It may also state the supporting documentation that you are requiring the obligor to bring. During the same visit, you must file an affidavit stating that you either attempted to execute on property belonging to the obligor or that you sent a demand letter and that you did not receive full or partial payment (item#13). The judge will then sign the order, and the clerk will give you a certified copy to serve upon the obligor. There are some states that will allow you to serve the obligor by certified letter; check with the court clerk before doing this.

On the day that you and your obligor must appear in court, the judge will call every debtor that is there to be examined. One by one, like a herd of cattle, they will be sworn in. After your obligor has given his/her oath you can then proceed to a quiet place (any quiet place will do) to proceed with your exam. If there are any documents or answers to your questions that need to be clarified, you can go into the courtroom and have the judge to make the final determination. During your exam you may discover that the obligor has some non-exempt assets. If you do,

MOTION FOR EXAMINATION OF JUDGEMENT DEBTOR

IN THE CIRCUIT COURT OF ANY STATE
FOR THE COUNTY OF ANY COUNTY

JANE DOE,	)	
Plaintiff	)	No. 0000
	)	
vs.	)	MOTION FOR EXAMINATION
	)	OF JUDGEMENT DEBTOR
JOHN DOE,	)	
Defendant	)	

Plaintiff moves for an order:

1. Requiring <u>Defendant John Doe</u> to appear at a time and place to be fixed by the court and answer under oath questions concerning any property or interest in property that defendant may have or claim, (and then and there to produce the following documents of the defendant:

_____

_____

_____

_____

2. Refraining defendant from selling, transferring or in any manner disposing of his (it's) property liable to execution, pending this proceeding.

3. This motion is based upon ORS 58.111, the records and the files herein, and (choose one) (either) the return service of an unsatisfied execution (or) proof of service on the attached affidavit of a notice of demand to pay the judgement within 10 days (or) proof of service on file herein of notice of demand to pay judgement with 10 days.

_____
Plaintiff

ITEM #11: MOTION FOR EXAMINATION OF JUDGEMENT DEBTOR

ORDER FOR EXAMINATION OF
JUDGEMENT DEBTOR

IN THE CIRCUIT COURT OF ANY STATE
FOR THE COUNTY OF ANY COUNTY

JANE DOE,	)	
Plaintiff,	)	No. 0000
	)	
vs.	)	ORDER FOR
	)	THE EXAMINATION
JOHN DOE,	)	OF JUDGEMENT DEBTOR
Defendant	)	

This matter coming on for hearing on plaintiff's motion for examination of judgement debtor, and it appearing form the records and files herein that the judgement in this matter is unsatisfied and (choose one) (either) an execution herein has been returned unsatisfied (or) a notice of demand to pay judgement within 10 days has been served upon defendant in a manner provided by law, it is hereby

ORDERED that John Doe appearing before the presiding judge of the above-entitled court in Room No. _____ of the Any County Courthouse, Any City, Any State, on the _____ day of _____, 1996 at the hour of _____, __.m., and answer under oath questions concerning any property or interest in property that defendant may have or claim, and it is further

ORDERED that Defendant be, and hereby is, restrained from selling, transferring, or in any manner disposing of any of his (her) (it's) property liable to execution pending this proceeding.

DATED this _____ day of August, 1996.

_____
CIRCUIT COURT JUDGE

ITEM #12: ORDER FOR EXAMINATION OF
JUDGEMENT DEBTOR

AFFIDAVIT IN SUPPORT OF MOTION

IN THE CIRCUIT COURT OF THE STATE OF ANY STATE
IN THE COUNTY OF ANY COUNTY

JANE DOE,
       Plaintiff)   No. 0000

       vs.)   AFFIDAVIT IN SUPPORT
)   OF MOTION

JOHN DOE,
       Defendant)

STATE OF ANY STATE)

County of Any County)

I, <u>Jane Doe,</u> being first duly sworn, depose and say that:

1. I am the Plaintiff.

2. On or about August 1, 1996, I caused a notice of demand to pay judgement to be deposited in the U.S. Mail postage prepaid, in a sealed envelope addressed to John Doe, defendant, at 1515 Deadbeat Lane, You Owe Me Money City, New Jersey, by certified mail, return receipt requested.

3. The notice of demand was served upon the defendant on <u>August 4, 1996,</u> as shown by the face of the receipt attached. (Attach a copy of the face of the receipt)

4. A true copy of the notice of demand is attached hereto, marked "Exhibit A," and by this reference made part hereof.

_____
                Plaintiff

SUBSCRIBED AND SWORN to before me this _____ day of August, 1996.

_____
NOTARY PUBLIC FOR NJ
My Commission Expires: _____

ITEM #13: AFFIDAVIT IN SUPPORT OF MOTION

go immediately to the judge when your exam is over and request that an order for the obligor to turn over the non-exempt items be issued. Item #14 is an example of some of the questions that you may want to ask your obligor.

CONTEMPT OF COURT

The person being charged with "Contempt of Court" faces jail time because they have not done what the court has ordered them to do. In your case, if your obligor is being charged with contempt, they have not paid their court ordered child support. Everyone is urged to utilize this method of child support collection, though it is not a cure-all. It may not work at all. Basically, what contempt of court will do is to drag the obligor into court to face the judge and explain why the child support payments have not been made. Rarely will a judge order jail time for an obligor with his/her first contempt of court charge. Usually obligors get far too many chances to pay before the judge will order a warrant for their arrest. If the obligor is arrested, child support must be paid before the obligor can be released.

That's where the system gets weak. It should be that the obligor is required to pay all of the back child support before they are let go. Anyone who has been through the process can tell you that is not the case. More often than not, the judge will release the obligor with a warning and require him/her to pay a portion of the child support before they are released.

Although the Contempt of Court proceeding leaves much to be desired, there are several reasons for suggesting that you use it. 1. If you only get 50 percent of what the obligor owes you, that's 50 percent more than you had before. 2. If you have to file repeated motions for contempt of court, eventually the judge will give the obligor jail time. 3. If you get nothing else you will get the satisfaction of seeing that the obligor was jailed. 4.I suggest that you employ every method that you can legally, physically, and mentally handle at one time. As the saying goes – if you throw enough mud on the wall, something has to stick.

A Contempt of Court proceeding is filed the same way any other motion is filed. Visit the clerks' office for the

SAMPLE QUESTIONS: FOR AN ORAL DEBTOR'S EXAMINATION OR WRITTEN INTEROGATORY

DATE: NAME OF COURT REPORTER, IF ANY

1. **Personal Information**
   A. Full Name:
   B. Residence address:
   C. Residence telephone number:
   D. Spouse's name, occupation, and employer:
   E. How many children under the age of 18?

2. **Occupation**
   A. Employer or name of business:
   B. Type of business:
   C. Your occupation:
   D. Business address:
   E. Business telephone number:
   F. Business associates:
   G. Name of employer's bank, address:
   H. Employment history for the past three years:

3. **Income**
   A. Income form occupation or business:
   B. Incomes from all other sources including pensions, disability, unemployment and other businesses:
   C. Commissions or renewals earned or anticipated:
   D. Pertinent information from state and federal tax returns and other books and records brought to the examination:

4. **Interests In Real Property**
   A. Beneficial or fee interest
   B. Amount of equity in home and who holds mortgage:
   C. Purchaser or seller on contract: With whom, how much is owed?:
   D. Lessor or lessee:
   E. Remainder or contingent interest:
   F. Beneficial use of any use of any real property in the name of another, including spouse:
   G. Mortgage or beneficiary under deed of trust:
   H. Any other interest whatever in any property in your state or any other state or country:

5. **Securities**
   A. Stock:
      1. If a shareholder in a close corporation, is the debtor an officer or director?

ITEM #14: SAMPLE QUESTIONS: FOR A DEBTOR'S EXAMINATION

          2. Who are the other officers, directors, and major
             shareholders?
          3. Any other stock?
          4. Any accounts with brokerage houses:
     B. Debt:
          1. Checks, drafts, or notes payable to the debtor:
          2. Bonds, dividends, certificates, certificates of deposit,
             deposits, or other interest- bearing instruments:

6.   **Cash Equivalent**
     A. Cash on hand:
     B. Safe Deposit Boxes:
     C. Bank, savings and loan, and credit union accounts of any kind:
     D. Deposits of money with any other institution or person:
     E. Cash value on insurance policies:
     F. IRS and state tax refunds due or expected:

7.   **Choses In Action**
     A. Accounts receivable or debts on open account
     B. Liquidated or unliquidated claims of any nature, including
        in contract and tort:
     C. Claims against insurance companies:
     D. Security interests and other liens or claims:

8.   **Other Personal Property**
     A. Household goods:
     B. Automobiles, trucks, motorcycles, and other vehicles:
     C. Boat or other vessel: How much is owed on it?
     D. Inventory, tools, machinery, and fixtures:
     E. Farm equipment, animals, or crops:
     F. Jewelry or other valuable property including sculpture,
        paintings, antiques, stamps, coins, etc.:
     G. Patents, copyrights, trademarks, trade names, royalties, etc.:
     H. Any documents of title, including warehouse receipts, etc.:
     I. Any interest in any other business, partnership, or joint venture:
     J. Real Estate listings:
     K. Any licenses or permits from public authorities:
     L. Any other property, tangible or intangible, which might have a
        potential value:

9.   **Trusts, Etc.**
     A. Is any property held for you in trust, guardianship, conservatorship,
        or custodianship?
     B. Are you a trustee, custodian, guardian or conservator?
     C. Are you an heir of anyone who has passed away?

10. **Legal Proceedings**
     A. Do you now have a legal claim against any party or does any party
        now have a legal claim against you?
     B. Have you been a party to any legal proceeding over the past three
        years?

ITEM #14: SAMPLE QUESTIONS: FOR A DEBTOR'S EXAMINATION, CON'T.

1. If so, have you satisfied any judgement against you?
2. Has there been a levy against any of your Property?
3. Has any third party satisfied any judgement for you?
4. Have you collected any judgement?

C. In the past three years, has the IRS or any state or county agency asserted a claim for unpaid taxes against you?

11.   Other Indebtedness

A. Names and addresses of secured creditors and amounts claimed by each:

B. Names and addresses of unsecured creditors and amounts claimed by each, including tax collectors: Names and addresses of judgement creditors, amount of each judgement:

C. Names and addresses of those to whom you have applied for a loan in the past 3 years:

12.   Transfers And Losses

A. Transfers of property within the past 2 years to relatives, charities, trusts, or others:

B. Money deposited in accounts in the name of another over the past 2 years:

C. Loans repaid over the past 2 years:

D. Assignments of payments, notes, contracts, insurance policies, or wages over the past 2 years: Example: purchases of property, including stock, for another over the past 2 years:

E. Transfers of any property over the past 2 years, not in the usual course of business:

F. Does anyone else hold title to or possession of any property in which you have any rights or interests?

13.   Books And Records

A. Name and address of accountant-bookkeeper:

ITEM #14: SAMPLE QUESTIONS: FOR A DEBTOR'S EXAMINATION, CON'T.

appropriate forms or pick them up at your supply store. You will need to simultaneously file a motion for an "Order to Show Cause" and an affidavit (items # 15 and 16). The motion for the "Order to Show Cause" states that the obligor must appear in court to explain the reasons why he/she should not be held in contempt for failing to pay child support. The affidavit will outline the reasons why they should be. You should attach a copy of your court order stating the amount of child support that was ordered, as well as a detailed account of missed payments and payments received, if any. These forms will need to be filed with the court clerk, who will tell you when to appear in court. You will receive a certified copy of the Order to Show Cause, (item #17) which must be served upon the obligor. Of course, you will keep a copy for yourself before you hand over the original.

At this point the case is very clear cut and unless the obligor can come up with some proof of payment he/she will be held in contempt. The only defense that he/she may have is that an illness or disability has prevented them from making the payments. Unemployment or underemployment is often used as a defense though it holds no legal grounds.

What happens from this point is purely potluck. It depends upon the judge that you are assigned, what his/her personal beliefs are and maybe the mood that they are in that day. The law allows for jail time for an obligor on his/her first contempt hearing. It allows the obligor to stay in jail until they are able to come up with the entire amount of back child support that they owe. None of this ever happens, however. Generally, they will be let off on a warning and a small amount of support paid. Unpaid child support will be considered arrearages and will be ordered to be paid off slowly. But holding the contempt hearing is better than not holding it. The threat of jail will continually hang over their head and if you have the kind of obligor that keeps you running back and forth to court on contempt charges, eventually their luck will run out.

MOTION AND AFFIDAVIT FOR ORDER
TO SHOW CAUSE RE: CONTEMPT

IN THE CIRCUIT COURT OF THE STATE OF ANY STATE
FOR THE COUNTY OF ANY COUNTY

In the Matter of:	)	
	)	No. 0000
JANE DOE,	)	
Petitioner	)	
	)	MOTION AND AFFIDAVIT
	)	FOR ORDER TO SHOW
and	)	CAUSE RE: CONTEMPT
JOHN DOE	)	
Respondent	)	

Petitioner moves for an order requiring the respondent to appear and show cause, if any there be, why petitioner should not be held in contempt of court for failing to comply with the provisions of the Judgement previously entered herein on or about August 1, 1996, as specifically alleged in the affidavit set forth herinbelow.

Petitioner declares that:

1. The maximum sanction the Petitioner seeks is an order incarcerating respondent in the county jail until he complies with the order of the court by paying child support to the Petitioner.

2. Petitioner seeks a sanction of confinement.

3. Petitioner considers this sanction to be remedial.

Petitioner also moves the court for Judgement against respondent on account of Petitioner's reasonable attorney fees and actual costs incurred herein supported by petitioner's affidavit as set forth herinbelow.

DATED this _____ day of August, 199_.

ITEM #15: MOTION AND AFFIDAVIT FOR ORDER TO
SHOW CAUSE RE: CONTEMPT

AFFIDAVIT

STATE OF NEW JERSEY   )
)

County of Ocean   )

I, _____, hereby swear the following to be true: I am the Petitioner herein. Respondent is my _____(former husband/boyfriend/wife/girlfriend). We were divorced pursuant to a Judgement and Decree of Dissolution of Marriage entered herein on or about August 1, 1996/ we ended our relationship on or about August 1, 1996 and a child support order was issued by the court on or about August 15, 1996.

Paragraph 4 of the court's Judgement reads as follows:

"4. That the respondent is hereby ordered to pay support to the Petitioner in the amount of $400 per month for the care, support and maintenance of said minor child, payable through the Essex County New Jersey Probation Department; Child Support Division in monthly payments of $400 each on the 1st of each month, until each child is emancipated in accordance with New Jersey State Law, and is no longer attending school on a regular basis. All support payments shall be in the form of cash or check made payable to Support Services, with the first such installment to be paid on or before August 16, 1996".

Respondent has failed and refused to pay any child support as ordered by the court despite repeated demand that he/she do so.

Based on the above, I believe respondent is in willful contempt of the decree of dissolution and therefore I ask that he/she be adjudged in contempt of court. In addition, I ask that the court impose all of the following sanctions, all of which I consider to be remedial in nature:

a. Requiring respondent to pay a sum of money sufficient to compensate me for loss, injuries, or costs suffered by me as a result of respondent's contempt of court.

b. Confining respondent in the Any County Jail or other appropriate facility for so long as his contempt continues, or six months whichever is shorter.

c. Requiring respondent to pay an amount not to exceed $500 or 1% of his annual gross income, whichever is greater, for each day that he/she remains in contempt of court. I ask the court that this sanction be imposed to compensate me for the effects of his/her continuing contempt.

d. Any order designed to insure compliance with a prior order of the court including probation.

e. Any other additional sanction if the court determines that the sanction would be an effective remedy for the contempt.

f. Awarding me judgement against respondent for all of my attorney fees, costs, and disbursements incurred in this matter.

_____, Petitioner

SUBSCRIBED AND SWORN to before me this _____ day of August, 1996.

_____
NOTARY PUBLIC   My Commission Expires: _____

ITEM #16: AFFADAVIT

ORDER TO SHOW CAUSE RE: CONTEMPT

IN THE CIRCUIT COURT OF ANY STATE
FOR THE COUNTY OF ANY COUNTY

STATE OF ANY STATE	)	
	)	No.000
JANE DOE	)	
Plaintiff,	)	
	)	ORDER TO APPEAR TO
vs.	)	ANSWER CONTEMPT OF
	)	COURT CHARGE – FAILURE
JOHN DOE	)	TO OBEY SUPPORT ORDER
Defendant.	)	
	)	

TO:

On the Motion of the Plaintiff,

YOU ARE ORDERED TO APPEAR in person before the Court, Any County Courthouse, 555 Pay The Money You Owe Avenue, New Jersey, and show cause why you should not be adjudged guilty of contempt of Court for disobeying the support order entered in the above-entitled Court and cause.

_____ BE PREPARED TO TESTIFY REGARDING
_____ YOUR FINANCIAL POSITION. BRING
_____ WITH YOU ANY RECORDS YOU MAY
_____ HAVE IN CONNECTION WITH YOUR
_____ INCOME, ASSETS, EXPENSES AND
_____ SUPPORT PAYMENTS.

NOTICE TO DEFENDANT: You are entitled to be represented by an attorney at the Court hearing. If you desire an attorney but cannot afford one, the Court will appoint legal counsel for you.

Dated this _____ day of August, 1996

_____
Circuit Court Judge

ITEM #17: ORDER TO SHOW CAUSE RE: CONTEMPT

Chapter 12: What The Government Can Do

There are other methods of collection that can be utilized to get child support that is in the arrears. These are methods that are only available to you through a government agency. You must have a current child support order and be using the state child support agencies to collect your child support in order for these government methods to work for you.

TAX REFUND INTERCEPT

Federal law allows for the interception of an obligor's federal tax refund if there is overdue child support in the amount of $150 or more. Think of it as a wage garnishment against a tax refund check. If you are receiving your child support through the state child support agency and you are due at least $150 from the obligor, tell your caseworker that you would like to have his/her tax refund intercepted. They will check to see if you have a child support order that is still in effect. If you do, you will be asked to sign an affidavit stating the amount of child support that is past due to you. They will also verify that they have the correct address for the obligor. If the address that they have is not current, it must be obtained before the intercept can take place.

When the address has been corrected, a letter is then mailed to the obligor advising him/her that their tax refund will be intercepted for the purpose of collecting past due child support. Advising the obligor of their intent to intercept allows them an opportunity to contest the action. If the obligor decides to contest the interception, he/she can only have two defenses that can hold up in court: 1. The obligor can object because they do not owe the amount of child support that is stated. In this case he/she would have to prove it by producing receipts of paid child support for the months that you say that it was not paid. 2. He/she can object because they are not the person that is named on the complaint. In this instance, the case of mistaken identity would have to be proved. Your obligor may feel that because he/she is making current on-time child support payments and is slowly paying off past due support, that their tax refund should not be intercepted. This is not the case, and it is not the law.

Unfortunately, most likely you will only be able to use the interception once as a means of getting past due child support. Once your obligor is on to you there is little chance that they will leave money in the hands of the federal government for you to get. Many obligors will at this time decide to change the status on their W-2 forms so that they don't overpay their taxes during the year. Instead they would rather owe the government and make their payment during tax time. Some may decide not to file their taxes at all.

If the obligor has filed their taxes with a new spouse the intercept will still be made. The non-obligor will then be able to contact the IRS and have the portion that is rightfully theirs refunded to them. Their portion will be determined by the amount of income that they showed on their income tax forms. (In the meantime, it would be nice to be a fly on the wall when that letter comes through).

The IRS intercept has accounted for more than 20% of all child support collected since 1981. The beauty of it is that it works like a charm, the down side is that it is not an automatically implemented tool - you must personally request that it be done. You must also request it many months in advance. Each state submits a case list to the IRS in August, along with the amount of the arrearages for an interception the following year; so you must plan far in advance. If your state or the state that your obligor lives in requires a state income tax to be filed, then check with your caseworker about intercepting that refund as well.

IRS COLLECTION PROCEDURE

This is a good method of collecting past due support, but like with every other method, it is not without it's down sides. For openers, your case must be handled by the state child support agency, or you must be on, or eligible, for welfare. Your case must be at least $750 in arrearages and it must be at least 6 months since you last asked for IRS collection assistance. Finally, you must provide identification information on the obligor and the IRS must have reason to believe that the obligor has assets that they can levy.

Once this checklist has been completed, someone from the IRS will attempt to contact the obligor to make a satisfactory arrangement. Sometimes the contact of an IRS agent is all a deadbeat needs to whip into shape. They will go out of their way to all-of-a-sudden find the money to pay you. After all, the IRS is involved now, suddenly child support seems like a serious issue. If IRS contact doesn't shape them up, the agent will the send a notice of intent to levy any and all unexempt property that the obligor may have. This is the same as you executing on the obligor's personal and real property, only the IRS is doing it now. Very few obligees use this IRS collection procedure and very few know that it exists. If your child support arrearages are on the high end and the assets that your obligor have are also on the high end, definitely use this method.

The IRS can also be used to locate the obligor and/or their assets. This can be done by doing a search on 1099 matches with names, social security numbers and wages. Those who are self-employed file 1099 forms with the IRS as opposed to W2 forms, for example. A 1099 is a means of reporting to the IRS your income and assets. If you have income from other sources outside of the wages that you earn (stocks, CD's, money markets, etc) it would be reported on a 1099 as well. It would also have the addresses that the obligor has reported to the outside source of income. This is useful because they may not report their correct address to the IRS if they know that you are after them. They may report the correct address to their income sources, however, so that they can receive their statements and quarterly reports.

Now, lets say that they are less than truthful when they are reporting to the IRS about their additional income sources. Maybe they don't list them all. They only list the ones that have old address information or that earn little money for them. The IRS has another procedure called the 1098. The 1098 reports to the IRS the interest that taxpayers pay on any certain account. So even if the obligor doesn't report it, the IRS has a way of finding it, and through that they may uncover a correct address or an asset gold mine.

As with most collection procedures, there are downsides to both the 1099 and the 1098 information and asset location. You can only request that these searches be done if previous information has been requested of the IRS but the obligor has still not been located. Also the information found can only be used for location purposes only, and can not be used to execute on found assets of the obligor. The way to get around this, however, is to subpoena the financial institution where the assets are located. They must at that time give you whatever information you request, even if it is information that you already have, but can't legally use.

Chapter 13: AFDC & Child Support

75% of women that are on AFDC (Aid for Families with Dependent Children [welfare]) receive public services because the absent parent of their children is unable or refuses to pay child support. In order to qualify for AFDC, normally you must not own a total of $1,000 in non-exempt property and have few resources and limited income. If you have any income at all while you are receiving public benefits it is deducted from your monthly allowance to insure that you pay the state back for any money that they give to you during your time of need. Consider it a signature loan. Just sign on the dotted line and you get the help that you need, but at some point in the future it must be paid back. If you own a home and are given an AFDC grant, the state will attach a lien on your property for the amount that you have been given. When you sell your house, you will have to pay back the money that you received while on welfare.

THE $50 DISREGARD
The only exception to this rule is the "$50 disregard".

The first $50 of any payment that you receive, per month, from any income source is disregarded as income. Child support is considered income, as is any money that anyone gives to you as a gift. If you are able to get a part-time job earning $75 per month, you will be allowed to keep the first $50 of that amount while the balance must be given to the state. Likewise, if you are able to get any child support from the obligor while you are on public assistance, you will get to keep the first $50. Whether the obligor makes the payment in full or only a partial payment for the month is irrelevant, you get the first $50 either way.

IN KIND PAYMENTS

If anyone makes payments on your behalf, say for your car, rent, or cable bill, they are not considered to be income unless the money touches your hands. If you are lucky enough to have someone that is willing to subsidize a better apartment for you or a safe vehicle to drive, have that person to make the payments directly. You are only permitted to keep the first $50 a month of any money that you come into direct ownership of. Payments made to your accounts by someone else on your behalf are called in-kind payments.

ASSIGNMENT OF RIGHTS

If you are on AFDC you have assigned the rights of your child support case to the state. This is true whether you came to the state with a child support order already in place or if they are helping you to establish an order. The state now has control of your case. You are no longer the beneficiary of your child support, the state is. They are the ones who will now decide what happens with it – or more appropriately – what doesn't happen with it. They have the right to decide what collection will be used to get money from your obligor and whether they want to decide to go after him/her at all. They can do this without consulting you. If they are receiving any child support at all, whether it is the full amount or not, whether they can get more or not, they may decide that they don't wish to pursue the case anymore and settle for the small amount of money that they get. To be fair, it should be noted that the state agencies have more cases than they can effectively handle. It stands to reason why everyone doesn't get the best care this way. But that doesn't do your case any good and there is absolutely nothing that you can do about it. You can jump up and down, scream and shout and tell your caseworker of the $400 a week raise that the obligor just got. If they don't want to pursue it, they don't have to. They own your case. You can't get a modification, wage garnishment, or take your obligor to court unless they say okay. What's worse, you may not be able to get the slightest bit of information on your case either.

When you apply for AFDC benefits they don't tell you that you are signing your rights away, though you are. If you had an attorney to represent you as you were signing up for benefits, she/he would have able to tell you exactly what you were signing. But of course, that's not the case since you needed every penny that you had at the time. I hate to be the bearer of bad news, but it's important that you know this before you try to start any kind of legal proceedings.

If you find yourself in this position you can only do two things: 1. Do nothing and accept your AFDC benefits. If you are on welfare, you must need the assistance. You probably can't afford to refuse benefits and pursue child support on your own. 2. If you strongly believe that you *can* handle your case better than the state has and you are willing to take the gamble of relinquishing your AFDC payments to pursue your child support – which could take months in some cases – then go for it. Many have succeeded this way.

The bottom line is this: you can't go after your obligor on your own if you are on welfare. Only you can decide if it will be worth your while to do without the benefits while you are chasing your deadbeat for money. If you are able to get child support from your obligor, will it be enough to sustain you? Will you be able to get it regularly or will you have to employ several collection methods to squeeze the money out of him/her? Find your answers, then make your best decision.

Chapter 14: Interstate Child Support Collection

It is much easier to collect child support if the obligor lives in the same state that you do. If you know where he/she lives and works, a wage withholding is an easy method of collecting your support payments. If you do not know where the obligor lives or works or if you need to do some "sleuthing" to find either the obligor or their assets, it's more difficult if he/she lives far away from you.

There are some commonly known and widely used collections techniques for obligors that do not live in the same state that you do.

INTERSTATE WAGE WITHHOLDING

The *Interstate Wage Withholding* is the most popular method of collection. It works the same way that a wage withholding works if the obligor lives in the same state that you do. The only difference is that you must cross state lines in order to collect the money. The *originating* state (the state that you live in) does not have *jurisdiction* over someone that does not live in their state, so they can not withhold his/her wages. Instead, your state must *petition* (ask) the state that the obligor lives in to withhold wages for child support and forward them to the state where you live. If the state child support collection agency were collecting your support for you, they would receive the payment and then forward it to you. If you were handling your own case, the payment would go directly to you.

The drawback with this method is that most states do not respond immediately when petitioned for help on a child support case. Often these procedures take months and can prove to be frustrating. The originating state is kept in the dark about whatever collection methods are, or are not, being used by the *responding* state. Generally, the *originating* state will send a *transmittal* by mail to the *responding* state once they have taken action on some collection method. But this is not guaranteed and even a small correspondence of this nature can take months on behalf of the *originating* state. Your caseworker and your state are left to wonder and so are you. Even though your caseworker can not take direct action on your child support case if it is out of state, the *Interstate Wage Withholding* is still the most effective method to use. Your decision at this point would then be whether you want to handle your case yourself, so that all of the correspondence must go to you, or do you want the state agency to handle your case for you.

If you want to file for an *Interstate Wage Withholding* yourself and you already have a child support order and a order for a wage withholding, you must provide the following documentation:

1. Certified copy of the original child support order
2. Certified copy of the order for a wage withholding
3. An affidavit from you testifying to the amount of arrearage and the supporting documentation that goes along with it or a certified copy of the payment record from the state agency that was collecting your support payments.
4. The full name and current address of the obligor
5. The name and address of the obligor's employer

6. The name and address of the *obligee* (you)

This information must be provided to the *responding state* in order to file a *foreign order* of support. A *foreign order* of support, simply stated, is a support order that you have obtained that you would like to enforce in another state. A child support order that you received in your state is not good in any other state unless you have it registered in the state where you will try to enforce it. If the obligor moves from state to state, you will have to register your child support order in each state before you attempt to collect on it. Think of it like a vehicle registration. Your car may be properly registered in your own state, but if you move to another state, you must have it registered there before you can consider it legally registered. Unfortunately, this is how our child support system works right now. This procedure to get a wage withholding on the income of an obligor that lives out of state is as follows:

1. Send the above documents to the withholding agency in the state where the obligor works. (Although most states will accept this documentation from you, there are some states that will only accept them from a government agency)
2. The support order will then be entered by the responding state.
3. You must then send notice to the obligor that you are intendingto withhold his/her wages. If you need to refresh you memory on how to do this, see Chapter 10.
4. As long as the obligor does not contest the wage withholding, an order will be sent to the obligor's employer.

These procedures can seem very complicated to most people. If you have any questions or are unsure about what do to at any time, you will probably be better off letting the state child support collection agency help you.

UNIFORM ENFORCEMENT OF FOREIGN JUDGEMENT ACT

A final judgement is a judgement for a sum that can not change; it is final. On-going child support payments are not final, they continue until the child reaches the age of majority. If you take an obligor to court for past due child support and win your case, a judgement will be entered for the amount of child support that is past due. That amount can not change. If the obligor continues to add arrearages, the amount that he/she owes you will continue to change, but the judgement amount will not. It is final. If you want to increase the judgement amount then you will have to return to court. If you have a final judgement for child support arrearages that you would like to collect, Under the Uniform Enforcement of Foreign Judgement Act, you can bring an action to enforce a foreign judgement in another state. Just as you must register a wage withholding in the new state before you can collect on it, you must register your judgement as well. The Uniform Enforcement of Foreign Judgement Act can only be used for final judgements. This is how you must proceed.

1. Call the clerk of the court where the obligor lives and ask they will accept a copy of a certified judgement, or must it be authenticated. Authenticated means that the clerk and judge of the originating state certify the document to be an authentic copy. By the responding clerk's standards, obtain a copy of the judgement and mail it to them.

2. File a statement giving the name and current address of the obligor.

3. The clerk will then notify the obligor that you have filed a foreign judgement and will supply a copy of the judgement

4. The obligor will then have up to 20 days (depending on the state) to contest the judgement. If he/she does not, you can then proceed with collection techniques.

NOTICE OF FILING OF FOREIGN JUDGEMENT

IN THE CIRCUIT COURT OF THE STATE OF ANY STATE
FOR THE COUNTY OF ANY COUNTY

In the matter of:)
JANE DOE   )   No. 000
    Petitioner   )   NOTICE OF FILING OF
)   FOREIGN JUDGEMENT
    and   )
JOHN DOE   )
)

      COMES NOW the petitioner and gives notice to respondent of the filing of the judgement rendered in the Circuit Court of the State of Any State on August, 1, 1994, a copy of which is attached hereto.

      DATED this _____ day of _____, 199_.

               _____
                   Jane Doe, Petitioner

AFFIDAVIT

STATE OF ANY STATE   )
)
County of Any County   )

      Jane Doe, Petitioner, makes this affidavit under oath.

      On August 1, 9994, a judgement was rendered by the Circuit Court of Any State styled "In re the Marriage of Doe in favor of Jane Doe against John Doe in the amount of $7,600".

      The name and last known address of the address of the Judgement Debtor is as follows:

      John Doe
      555 Deadbeat Lane
      Deadbeat, NJ

      Jane Doe
      You Owe Me Lane
      Money, NJ

      SIGNED this 3rd day of August, 1994

               _____
                   Jane Doe, Petitioner

ITEM #18: NOTICE OF FILING OF FOREIGN JUDGEMENT

UNIFORM RECIPROCAL ENFORCEMENT OF SUPPORT ACT (URESA)

URESA is a law that allows you to file for current child support, back support, a modification of your child support award, medical expenses, and custody/visitation, without leaving your own state. It is the same as applying for services through your local child support agency asking them to collect support due from someone that lives in the same state that you do. The difference is that URESA only handles interstate cases. When you petition through URESA, they will file your documentation with the obligor's state and have someone to represent you at the hearing where the absent parent/obligor resides.

You can apply for services from URESA through your state child support collection agency. At that time you will be assigned a caseworker who will be your main source of communication between yourself and the responding state.

You can also apply yourself, or through an attorney, by calling the Family Court in your area and asking them where you must go in your area to apply for services.

LONG ARM STATUTES

Many people do not know about *Long Arm Statutes,* though if they did, they could eliminate a lot of the heartache that goes along with collecting across state lines. If your obligor lives out of state, you must have your judgement(s) registered in the state where the obligor lives before you can attempt to collect any money. Let's say that not only does your obligor live out of state but also has a vacation house in the same state that you live in. If that were the case, you would not have to have the judgement(s) registered in the other state, because the obligor has legal residence in the state where the judgement was written. If the obligor lived in another state, but worked in your state, the same would apply. Now let's say that the obligor lives 2,500 miles away and works in the same state that he/she lives in. The company that he/she works for is a large company and they have branches in over 25 states; one of those branches is in the state where you live. Since your state has jurisdiction over the company

135

that is doing business in your state, it can order the company to do many things; one of those things is to pay your child support. In a case like this you could save yourself the time of registering your judgement somewhere else in order to get your support money.

Long Arm Statutes can vary from state to state. Though they may not be universally accepted, it can't hurt you to try. The most you can get out of it is to collect your child support, the least it can get you is nothing, which is what you have right now.

Chapter 15: Collecting From The Self Employed

If your obligor is self-employed, you have a unique set of issues and problems when it comes to child support enforcement. The self-employed obligor can not have his/her wages withheld, because, under the law, technically he/she does not earn "wages". When you take him/her to court for child support, you may not be able to get a fair amount of support in proportion to his/her earnings because he/she may not legally report all business earnings. Unless you do some research, you may not even know that the obligor is running a business at all.

When it comes to self-employed obligors that don't want to pay, you have to pull out the heavy artillery. Strict enforcement techniques that have been outlined in Chapters 10, 11, and 12, will have to be used to collect from the unyielding self-employed obligor. Assuming that you have utilized all methods that you could (or are in the process of doing so presently) the following are some methods that you can use to take money directly from the obligor's business.

BANK ACCOUNTS

If the obligor is operating a sole-proprietorship, he/she is using his/her own social security number for business tax records. Since that is the case, anything that the business owns, the obligor owns as well. You can garnish business accounts that have cash available.

BUSINESS PROPERTY

You can also seize and sell business property. For example, if the obligor is running a local mechanics shop that has equipment worth a lot of money, re-read Chapter 10 and go to work on a seize and sell. Company equipment is not the only items that can fall prey to be seized and sold. Any kind of office equipment, inventory and furniture can be seized for the payment of child support.

TILL TAP

If the obligor is running a business with a cash register, have the sheriff conduct a till-tap. Remember to wait until the busiest season and the busiest time of day to reap the most benefit from this.

BUSINESS SUPPLIERS

If you are fortunate enough to know whom some of the obligor's suppliers are, you are ahead of the game. If you do not know the suppliers do some research to find out. Then subpoena them for whatever information that you can. If you find that the obligor is paying for shipments of goods, you can place a lien on whatever shipment(s) that the obligor has paid for. Of course, the obligor will be as mad as a lunatic, but alas, that is what you want. He/she will have no other choice but than to pay you so that you release the lien, or watch his/her business go down the tubes. (You will, of course, attach a lien on every shipment with every supplier that he/she has until you are paid in full).

If the shoe is on the other foot and your obligor is the supplier; you can garnish the payment that the obligor is due to receive from the company that the obligor shipped the goods to.

The previous collection methods listed under "Business Suppliers" are methods that used leverage over the obligor. If you have leverage, the obligor may be willing to give you what you want just to get you off of his/her back. Some examples of leverage may be:

1. If you are certain that the obligor is not reporting a portion of their income, you can threaten to gather proof and call the IRS.
2. If the obligor is an immigrant and his/her Visa has expired, you can threaten to call immigration.

You know the obligor better than I do. Find his/her soft spot and then "go for the jugular". Don't hold back and don't feel badly that you have caused so much misery for him/her. He/she isn't exactly feeling sorry for you and your children when you eat soup for supper every night. If that were the case, you would have the child support that you need.

Chapter 16: Collecting From The Unemployed & Underemployed

There are many obligees that complain that they can not get any child support from their obligor, because he/she does not have a job; they are unemployed. There are others that complain that they can not get enough child support or that the arrearages will never go away, because, the obligor does not make enough money. They say that they can not get blood from a stone. And I say that they have not learned the best way to squeeze. In more instances than not, though it may be a long wait at times, you can get child support-even from an unemployed obligor. The following items outline some of the many ways you can cash in on "other incomes" to get child support from someone that is unemployed or underemployed.

1. Unemployment – In most states a portion of an obligor's unemployment benefit can be withheld for child support.

2. Disability - If the obligor is receiving disability benefits you and/or your child may be entitled to benefits as well. Contact your local Social Security office for an appointment to find out.

3. Veteran's Benefits – Contact the regional office closest to you. In most instances, veteran's benefits can not be held for child support. There are some complicated exceptions to this rule, so before you decide not to bother contact them and let them figure it out for you. If you have an attorney involved, of course, seek his/her assistance as well.

4. Life Insurance Policies – If the obligor has a life insurance policy that can be eventually cashed in, that policy can be garnished for past due support and withheld for future support payments depending on the amount of the policy.

5. Assets – If the obligor has assets that are worth you going through the trouble of seizing and selling (especially real estate) move to have a lien placed on the property and foreclose if it comes to it

6. Inheritance – This may seem morbid, but if you can't get any money from the obligor, you may get some from his/her parents or someone else that may leave him/her money in a will. If you continually update your judgement in court so that the proper amount is reflected at the time you can collect the money, you will be able to receive interest from day one to the day you get your child support. Be sure to ask to judge for pre-judgement interest as well as post-judgement interest.

7. Lottery Winnings – You don't have to be in it to win it. New Jersey and California have begun to attach the lottery winnings of those who owe child support.

Of course, these are only some of the ways that you can get blood from your own stone. If you think about it for awhile, considering what you know about the obligor, I'm sure that you can think of some yourself.

Chapter 17: Collecting From The Military

If you are trying to collect child support from someone that is in the military, there is good news and there is bad news. The good news is that the military has polices toward family support and the policies are good ones. Each branch of the military which includes the Army, Navy, Air Force, Marines, and Coast Guard insist that their personnel support their families back home. The bad news is that it can be difficult to locate a military employee at times and when you do, their superior officers are not always as helpful as they should be.

If you know where the obligor is stationed, half of your battle is over. Write a letter to the soldier's commanding officer. Let him/her know that you have a judgement for a child support order. Supply your name, address, and a copy of the judgement, the soldier's name and his/her service number. Request that the commanding officer assist you in obtaining your support.

In some instances the commanding officer will help you by having the appropriate amount of child support withheld from the soldier's pay (without a wage withholding order) and forwarded to you. In other instances you will be sent away and told to obtain a wage withholding prior to being helped. Unfortunately you can not send a wage withholding to the Military yourself; it will not be accepted. You must use the services of the child support agencies. Once the wage withholding is received at the proper branch, you can expect to get payments after 60 days.

If you do not want to use the child support agencies and are not getting any help from the soldier's commanding officer, there are other people that you can contact who may help. If you are in a bind and need immediate financial assistance, contact the Red Cross and/or the Army Relief Fund. These organizations have emergency funds available to assist the families of military employees. You will need to provide your child support order, your name and address, and the soldier's name, address, and service number, if you have it. Also contact the *Inspector's General*. The *Inspector's General* is someone that can put pressure on the obligor's Commanding Officer for not doing his/her job properly, and can get your money on it's way to you quickly.

If you do not have a judgement for a child support order and you are married (and the law can assume paternity) but separated from your spouse, you may be able to get child support anyway. Ask the commanding officer when you write to him/her.

If you do not know where the obligor is stationed you can find out by contacting the recruitment office where the obligor enlisted. This information is a matter of public record. If you know where the obligor has been assigned, call the "installation locator" at that particular installation. Then call the number that you are given and ask for the soldier's unit of assignment.

If you still have not been able to locate the solider, try the military locator services located in the back of this book.

Chapter 18: Collecting Internationally

Collecting child support is difficult if you have to cross state lines. Imagine the difficulty you will have if you have to cross borders or oceans to other countries to collect your support payments. The United States is not the only country that has to deal with issues of child support or child support enforcement. Luckily for you, other countries have this problem as well. Because of this, and because their citizens sometimes cross the border into the United States seeking refuge from having to pay child support, they are, at times, willing to set up agreements between us to enforce foreign child support orders.

There are no formal agreements between the U.S. and other countries for the payment of child support, although there are some countries that the U.S. has reciprocity with, and others that we are developing. Many of the 50 states have been utilizing URESA for the collection of child support in other countries. Under URESA, a child support judgement from the United States is treated as a foreign judgement in another country. Once it is registered, the responding jurisdiction (in this case, the foreign country) will reciprocate by using URESA practices to sue the obligor for child support or enforce the existing order. As you learned in Chapter 14, if this action were to take place between two states it would be considered the enforcement of a Foreign Judgement Act. Between two countries it is *Comity*. *Comity* is the practice of a country recognizing the law of another country within it's own jurisdiction.

This is not to say that all countries will allow comity. There are a few countries that will allow the enforcement of a foreign child support order, but there are also many that will not. The rule of thumb is that if the country has the same or a "substantially similar law" in effect, they will probably allow comity.

Arrangements have been made with the following countries:

Canada	Sweden
France	Hungary
United Kingdom	Poland
Norway	

The following countries have arrangements in process:

Israel	Belgium
Italy	Denmark
Austria	Czechoslovakia
Spain	Yugoslavia
Portugal	The Netherlands

I'm sorry to say that if your obligor has fled the country, you have a long road ahead of you when it comes to child support collection. If you have the money, the best thing that you can do in this situation is to hire an attorney in the country where the obligor has fled (remember the home court advantage). If you are able, also hire an attorney in your state to represent you here. If you do not have the means to hire an attorney or two, use the services of the child support enforcement agencies.

Chapter 19: Collecting From A Federal Employee

Collecting child support from a civilian federal employee can be one of the worst things you can attempt to do. The government makes it difficult, if not impossible, for anyone to attempt to get money involuntarily from one of its own. They will return court documents unanswered if information they want was not included. When they do allow a garnishment they will only allow it to be taken from the employee's net (take home) pay, which includes other deductions like retirement, life insurance, savings plans etc., rather than the employees gross pay. Once all deductions have been made, there may not be anything left to garnish. When serving a federal employee, if the documents are not sent to the proper office, to the proper person, they will be returned. At the same time, the government has laws that state that federal employees can not be indebted to anyone or any entity. The best thing you that you can do when you are dealing with the federal government, or one of it's employees, is to use the government laws to your advantage when you can and beat them at their own game.

1. Prior to serving a wage withholding, visit your local library and ask the reference librarian to help you find Code Federal Regulations # 5 CFR Part 581. This is where you will the address for every executive federal branch. Locate the branch that your obligor works in. You will be able to use the address you have found to properly serve him/her.

2. Mail the wage withholding return receipt certified mail from the post office. Expect to pay a small fee of about $3.00 for this service. Along with your wage withholding, include the obligor's name, date of birth, social security number, civil service retirement number (if there is one), veteran's claim number (if there is one) and advise of the office where he/she works. Also include your name, address, a copy of the judgement, and the purpose of the judgement.

3. If you want to circumvent the system, contact the civilian employees' supervisor by mail and request his/her assistance collecting your support. Gently remind him/her that Code Federal Regulation 5 CFR Part 735.207 prohibits the indebtedness of federal employee's and subjects them to discipline for failure to pay his/her debts. Also remind him/her that Code Federal Regulations 5 CFR Part 735.209 prohibits conduct by a federal employee that may be prejudicial to the government. This may get you some action from the supervisor. Of course, in order for an employee to be disciplined for failing to pay his/her debts, it must somehow interfere with the employees job performance. And, of course, it will, if the employee has to go to court several times for the non-payment of child support.

If the obligor is not a federal employee, but does business with the federal government by way of contract, you are out of luck. Government contractors are exempted from garnishments of any kind. Other methods of child support collection outlined in Chapters 10-13 will have to be utilized.

Chapter 20: When An Obligor Files For Bankruptcy

When I was working in collections for the bank, the person I was collecting from often told me that he/she was in bankruptcy. If a person files for bankruptcy, all collection attempts must stop immediately. This is called an "automatic stay". If they continue it can be construed as harassment and there can be penalties. This is true when it comes to child support collection as well. If the obligor files for bankruptcy, you can no longer pursue child support collection until you go to court to apply for a "relief" from the "stay".

A person, or a company, can file for bankruptcy to either have all of his/her debts discharged (eliminated), or to have a "stay" from the collection procedures until the debts can be slowly paid off over time. Child support can not ever be discharged, but it can be paid off at a slower pace. If your obligor has filed for bankruptcy, it will be handled in one of the following ways:

Chapter 7: Is the bankruptcy type where all of the debts are discharged. The obligor starts off with a clear slate with no debts. Child support is an *undischargeable* debt. Seek immediate relief from the bankruptcy court by using the following motion.

Chapter 11: Is mostly for businesses that are in over their heads. They can propose a *reorganization* to the bankruptcy judge where they outline how their debts will be paid off. If the judge says it's okay, they then go into a Chapter 11. If the judge does not accept their proposal, then the bankruptcy becomes a Chapter 7.

Chapter 13: Is similar to the Chapter 11, but it is for individuals. It works the same way in that the individual filing for a bankruptcy must outline show all outstanding debts will be paid. If accepted the individual can keep his/her personal property, if not, it is liquidated.

In all three instances you are entitled to a relief from the stay. If the obligor has filed for a Chapter 13, all past child support owed will be reorganized under the plan. You can not continue to attempt collection on that amount. Current child support and future child support can not be reorganized so those full amounts are still due to you. For example, if the obligor filed for bankruptcy on the first of the month owing you $3,000 with $500 due the first of every month, he/she would still owe you $500 when the next month rolls around. The past due $3,000 would be *reorganized* with the bankruptcy judge and you would have to accept whatever payment arrangement the judge accepts.

To file a relief from a stay it will cost about $70 and it can be filed at the clerks' office. Remember to serve a copy to the obligor, his/her attorney, if there is one, and the trustee. The notice that you receive informing you of the obligor's upcoming bankruptcy proceeding will provide you with the names and addresses of the people that you need to serve.

Chapter 21: Effective Complaining

When all else fails and the child support enforcement agency is not doing their job to their fullest potential, you can always complain. Complaining in an inefficient manner, or to the wrong people, will not get you anywhere. Complaining effectively, will. This chapter is about learning how to effectively complain, and how to complain to people who can help you.

Before considering a complaint to anyone be sure that you have accurate records to support your positions; be attentive in your record keeping. Here is a list to help you keep impeccable records.

1. Keep a log of every conversation that you have with caseworker or anyone else that you may speak to at the agency. The log should state what was said during the conversation, what action the caseworker promised and when he/she told you to follow up (after you asked). It should also have the date and time that the conversation took place. Case log example:

2/20/98 9:30 a.m. Spoke with Marti, she said that she does not have any new information. I told her that I was able to locate Dan's new home address and work address. She said that she will get to work on a wage withholding. I will follow up with her in 2 weeks.

3/7/98 9:45 a.m. Marti says that she hasn't had time to do a wage withholding because she has so many cases to work on. She told me to follow up with her in 2 weeks.

3/21/98 3:25 p.m. Marti was not at her desk, so I left a message.

3/21/98 4:00 p.m. Marti was not at her desk, so I left a message.

3/22/98 9:05 a.m. Marti said that she would check into the matter, but she didn't get back to me as she promised. I faxed a letter to her and her supervisor.

3/23/98 10:40 a.m. Glenda, Martys' supervisor returned my call to say that a wage withholding has been put into effect.

The case log has showed many things. It gives an account of what transpired between client and caseworker. In this way you won't have to rely on your memory to put details together; you will also be better informed. By having the accurate dates of when you spoke with your caseworker the last time, you won't let too much time go by without a necessary phone call. The time of day that you normally reach your caseworker gives you an indication of when he/she is likely to be reachable.

2. Keep copies of anything and everything that you must forward to your caseworker, whether it is information on the obligor or a complaint letter that you sent to the caseworker or supervisor.

3. When sending a complaint letter to your caseworker or the caseworker's supervisor, send it by fax if you

have one available to you. A faxed document will get to your caseworker immediately, rather than waiting for "snail mail" through the post office. If you don't have a fax machine accessible to you, use the regular mail service.

4. If you must send a complaint letter to someone higher than your caseworker supervisor, send it by fax, but also send it return receipt certified mail from the post office. You will get a notice in the mail of when your letter was received at the child support agency and they will know that you mean business.

5. Every letter that you send to your caseworker should be carbon copied to the caseworker's supervisor. At the bottom of the letter that you are sending, underneath your signature, type "cc: (supervisor's name)", and then send a duplicate of the letter to the supervisor. This accomplishes two things, first it lets the caseworker know that you are keeping his/her supervisor informed, and second it advises the supervisor of all on-goings with the case. In the event that you will have to complain, the supervisor should not be surprised and should be well equipped to handle it.

6. When you do get action on your case that was promised, be sure to write a quick thank you note to whomever it was that brought about the action.

When considering complaints, the chain of command should go like this:

1. First complain to the caseworker. (Item #19) If you are able to speak with him/her ask when would be a good time to follow up. Do not get off the phone without asking for a follow-up date no matter what they say. Do not let him/her blow you off. Unless he/she is waiting for action from a responding state, a follow-up date generally should be no more than 2

weeks later. If the caseworker does not respond to you at all, wait two weeks before you take the next step.

2. If the caseworker does not do as they promised, or if you are otherwise unhappy with the results that you have gotten, complain to the caseworker's supervisor. (Item #20) If caseworkers supervisor also does not prove to be helpful, wait two weeks before you take the next step up the rung.

3. The Assistant Chief Probation Officer is the next person that you would contact. He/she is the manager over the supervisors in the child support enforcement office, followed by the Chief Probation Officer himself/herself. Telephone contact is usually the first methods of contact, followed by any letters that you will send. If you end up sending a letter to the Assistant Chief Probation Officer, be sure to also cc: both the caseworker, and the caseworker's supervisor, so that they can expect to hear from the big boss. In my experience, many cases do not go beyond the Assistant Chief. If yours does, the appendix section in the back of this book will have the proper chain of command. In addition to contacting the proper officials, who can get action on your case within the child support enforcement offices, also contact your elected officials. (Item #21) Elected officials can put pressure on the child support enforcement office to get the job done. Begin with your Congressperson and/or Senator.

Not only must you know the proper people to speak/write to, you must also know the best way to write a complaint letter so that it gets the attention it deserves. Many obligees write long letters about how her/his ex left home, kicked the dog, smacked the kids, and took off in the car. Sorry to say, but the caseworker isn't interested in your sob story. There are about a hundred that comes across his/her desk every day and half of them are probably worse than yours. The only information that your caseworker is interested in is the facts. Be short and sweet, but firm. Examples of complain letters:

Date

Caseworker
Name Of Child Support Agency
Street Address
City, State, Zip
Re: Case Number - 987456985

Dear Caseworker:
    I spoke with you last week on (date), and you promised me that you would have a wage withholding done on my case. We agreed that I should follow up today. When I called your office you told me that you had not had a chance to do the wage withholding because you have so many cases. Since you promised to do this last week and did not do so, please be certain to do it now. I have been waiting far too long for my child support. If you need to reach me, please call me at home, 617-555-5555. Thank you for your time.

    Sincerely,

    Margie Bennett

cc: Glenda Fidel, Supervisor

ITEM #19: SAMPLE COMPLAINT LETTER TO CASEWORKER

Date

Caseworker
Name Of Child Support Agency
Street Address
City, State, Zip
Re: Case Number 326547986

Dear Assistant Chief Probation Officer,

   I have become very frustrated with the progress on my case and with your agency. I am not receiving any action on my case, and I do not get a response from my caseworker or my caseworker's supervisor when I call or when I write.

   At this time I am requesting a copy of my case log so that I can see what activity has taken place on my case. I am also asking that a wage withholding be done on the obligor's income. I provided my caseworker with this information a month ago. Thank you for your time.

   Sincerely,

   Margie Bennett

cc: Toni Jones, Caseworker
      Glenda Fidel, Supervisor

ITEM #20: SAMPLE COMPLAINT LETTER TO CASEWORKER'S SUPERVISOR

Date

Government Official
Street Address
City, State, Zip

Dear Government Official:

Enclosed you will find correspondence between the Child Support Enforcement Agency and myself. As you will see I have not had much action on my case and I have provided everything that I can to the agency. It has been 120 days since I have asked them to run a state and a federal locator to find a current address for my former husband. Although the law provides for 75 days to conduct a search, they still have not gotten back to me. Telephone calls and letters to their office remain unanswered.

Please help me with my case.

Sincerely,

Margie Bennett

cc: Chief Probation Officer, Samuel Barnes
        OceanGate County Child Support Office
        Street Address
        City, State, Zip

**ITEM #21: SAMPLE COMPLAINT LETTER TO
ELECTED OFFICIAL**

Appendix A: Glossary

Abnormal specimen testing- A method of paternity testing that can be done on a deceased body to determine DNA matching for paternity

Absent parent- A parent that does not live with their children, but that has financial responsibility for them. Also known as the non-custodial parent

AFDC/ADC (Aid to Families with Dependent Children)- Financial assistance (welfare) for families who have children that are deprived of the financial support of one of their parents by reason of death, disability, or continued absence

Affidavit- A written declaration, or statement of fact, made under oath, or in the presence of an officer authorized to make declarations under oath

Arrearages- Unpaid child support payments owed by a parent that has been ordered to pay

Appeal- To request that a case be transferred to another court, for a higher hearing

Automatic stay- The process by which a legal proceeding in progress must immediately come to an end

Buccal swab sampling- A method of DNA matching, for the purpose of determining paternity, in which a large cotton swab is brushed along the inside of the cheek, collecting skin cells that can be tested for matching DNA

Change in circumstances- A change in the financial circumstances of either the non-custodial or the custodial parent, deeming the present child support order unfair

Child Support Enforcement Agency- A state run government agency that collects child support payments for custodial parents

Child support award- An amount of money that a non-custodial parent has been ordered by a court of law to pay for the upkeep of his/her children

Comity- The practice by which one state or country recognizes the judgements or decisions of another though they do not legally have to. It is a show of good faith

Consent agreement- Voluntary written admission of paternity, or responsibility of child support

Court Ordered- A terminology used when an officer of the court has made a decision and handed down a ruling

Creditor's bill- A legal motion that must be filed with the court to prove that a person or entity is in possession of property that belongs to another person or entity

Credit reporting agency- An agency that reports one's timely and late indebtedness to others, for the purpose of establishing credit worthiness

Custodial parent- Parent with whom child lives, and who has legal custody of the child

Custody- Legal determination that establishes with whom a child should live

Default- Failure of a defendant to file an answer, response, or appeal in a civil case within a certain number of days, after having been served with a summons and complaint

Default judgement- Decision made by the court when the defendant fails to respond

Defendant- The person against whom a civil or criminal proceeding is begun

Deposition- A question and answer period that is conducted under oath

Discharged- The terminology used in bankruptcy when a debt is eliminated

DNA matching- A method of familial relationship determination in which genetic chromosomal material is matched for it's hereditary pattern

Downward Modification- The terminology for a previously awarded child support amount being lowered

Enforcement- Forcing the payment of a child support or medical support obligation

Establish paternity- The process of having paternity proved and established in a court of law

Estoppel- A law that says that once a decision has been made in a court of law, you can not go back and ask that it be changed based on information that you had when the decision was made

Execution- Enforcement of a civil money judgement by ordering a sheriff to seize and sell the debtor's real or personal property

Family Calculation- A method of DNA matching for the purpose of paternity testing in which immediate family members of the suspected father are matched along with the child in question. This is normally done when the suspected father is not available for DNA matching

Federal Parent Locator Service (FPLS)- A service provided by the federal government through the Office of Child Support Enforcement (OCSE) for the purpose of searching Federal Government records to locate absent parents

Foreign order- A judgement that was determined in a state or country other than your own

Forensic paternity testing- Methods of DNA matching for the purpose of paternity that can be done in the absence of the suspected father

Garnishee- The person, or entity, in possession of property that belongs to a debtor upon whom a garnishment is served

Garnishment- A legal proceeding whereby a portion of a person's wages, or other assets, is withheld and applied to payment of a debt

Guidelines- Standard methods for setting child support obligations based on the income of the parent(s) and other factors as determined by State law.

Hearing- An appearance before a judge, hearing officer or administrative other

Indigent- A person who is poor or needy

Initiating state- The state in which a proceeding is commenced and where the custodial parent is located

Interstate case- A child support case in which the custodial parent and the non-custodial parent live in two different states

Interstate wage withholding- A child support case in which a wage withholding is sent from one state to another to be processed

Judgement- A legal decision made by the court. Also known as an order

Jurisdiction- Legal authority which a court has over particular persons, certain types of cases, and in a defined geographical area

Legal father- A man that is recognized by law as the male parent

Legislation- The making of laws

Letter of consent- Voluntary written admission of paternity or responsibility for support

Leverage- The use of power or effectiveness to enhance one's capacity

Lien- A claim upon property to prevent sale or transfer until a debt is satisfied

Long arm statute- A law that permits one State to claim personal jurisdiction over someone who lives in another State

Medical support- A legal provision for payment of medical and dental bills – can be linked to a parent's access to medical insurance

Modify- To change

Motion- An application to a judge for an order or a hearing

Non-AFDC case- A case where an application for child support enforcement has not been filed and the family is not receiving public assistance

Non-Custodial parent- The parent who does not have primary custody of a child but who has a responsibility for financial support

Obligation- Amount of money ordered by the court to be paid by the responsible parent and the manner by which it is to be paid

Obligee- A custodial parent or guardian that has been awarded a child support order by the court

Obligor- A non-custodial parent that has been ordered by the court to pay child support

Offset- An amount of money taken from a parent's State or Federal income tax refund to satisfy a child support debt

Order- A judgement handed down from a judge or other officer of the court

Originating state- The State from which legal documents originate

Paternity- Male parentage

Paternity judgement- Legal determination of fatherhood

Paternity test- A test that can determine male parentage

Plaintiff- A person who brings an action, complains, or sues in a civil case

Pro-Se'- The act of representing yourself during a court proceeding

Public Assistance- Money granted to individuals or families for living expenses; based on need

Responding State- A state receiving and acting on an interstate child support case

Retainer- A fee paid to retain an attorney's services

Serve (service of process)- The delivery of a summons or other notice to a person or entity

Show cause- A court order directing a person to appear and bring evidence to offer reasons why a court order should not be executed. A show cause order is usually based upon a motion and affidavit asking for relief

State Parent Locator Service (SPLS)- A service operated by the State to locate absent parents

Subpoena- An official document ordering a person to appear in court or to bring and/or send documents

Summons- A notice to a defendant that an action against him/her has been commenced

Title IV-D- Title IV-D of the Social Security Act is the portion covering the child support enforcement program

Title IV-D Agency- A State agency that collects child support for custodial parents under Title IV-D

Transcript- A typewritten copy of a deposition

Undischargeable- A debt that can not be discharged under the bankruptcy law

Unearned income- Income that a person or entity receives that has not been earned by way of employment

Upward Modification- The terminology for a previously awarded child support amount being increased

URESA (Uniform Reciprocal Enforcement Support Act)- A law which allows a custodial parent that lives in one State to establish and enforce a child support order against a non-custodial parent that lives in another State

Visitation- The right of a non-custodial parent to visit or spend time with his/her children

Volunteer agreements- An agreement made between a custodial parent and a non-custodial parent for the payment of child support; made in lieu of a formal child support order

Wage withholding- Procedure by which automatic deductions are made from wages or income to pay a debt such as child support; may be voluntary or involuntary

Writ- An order issuing from a court and requiring the performance of a specific act, or giving authority and permission to have it done

Written interrogatory- A deposition that is conducted through the mail

Appendix B: State Child Support Enforcement Offices

As Of February, 1999

ALABAMA
Bureau of Child Support
Dept. of Human Services
50 Ripley
Montgomery, AL 36130
1-800-284-4347

ALASKA
Child Support Enforcement Div.
Dept. of Revenue
550 West 7th Ave., 4th Fl.
Anchorage, AK
(907) 269-6900

ARIZONA
Child Support Enforcement Admin.
Dept. of Economic Security
P.O. Box 6123/Site Code 776-A
2222 W. Encanto
Phoenix, AZ 85005
(602) 252-4045

ARKANSAS
Officer of Child Support Enforcement
Arkansas Social Services
P.O. Box 8133
Little Rock, AR 72203
(501) 682-8398

CALIFORNIA
Division of Child Support
Department of Social Services
744 P Street/Mail Stop 9-011
Sacramento, CA 95814
(916) 657-3661

COLORADO
Division of Child Support
Department of Social Services
1575 Sherman Street
Denver, CO 80203-1714
(303) 866-5994

CONNECTICUT
Bureau of Child Support
    Enforcement
Dept. of Human Resources
1049 Asylum Avenue
Hartford, CT 06105
(800) 228-5437

DELAWARE
Division of Child Support
Dept. of Health & Social Services
920 King Street
New Castle, DE 19720
(302) 573-6447

DISTRICT OF COLUMBIA
Office of Paternity & Child
Support
Department of Human Services
800 9th Street S.W. 2nd Floor
Washington, D.C. 20001
(202) 724-8800

FLORIDA
Office of Child Support
    Enforcement
Dept. of Health & Rehabilitative
1317 Winewood Blvd. Bldg. 3
Tallahassee, Florida 32399-0700
(850) 488-4975

GEORGIA
Office of Child Support Recovery
State Dept. of Human Resources
878 Peach Tree N.E.
Atlanta, GA 30309
(404) 654-3880

HAWAII
Child Support Enforcement
    Agency
Department of Attorney General
Box 1860
Honolulu, HI 96805
(808) 548-5326

IDAHO
Bureau of Child Support Enforcement
Department of Health & Welfare
450 W. State Street, 6th Floor
Pete T. Cenarrusa Building
Boise, ID 83702
(208) 334-5710

ILLINOIS
Bureau of Child Support Enforcement
Illinois Department of Public of
    Public Aid
Bloom Building
P.O. Box 19405, 20L.S.
Grand Avenue. E.
Springfield, IL 82705
(217) 782-1366

INDIANA
Child Support Enforcement Division
Department of Public Welfare
402 N. Washington Street
Room W360
Indianapolis, IN 46204
(317) 232-4885

IOWA
Bureau of Collections
Iowa Department of Human Services
727 E. 2nd Street
Des Moines, IA 50309
1-888-229-9223

KANSAS
Child Support Enforcement
Program
Dept. of Social & Rehabilitation
Services
P.O. Box 497
Topeka, KS 66601-0497
(785) 296-3237

KENTUCKY
Department of Child Support
Enforcement
Department of Social Insurance
Cabinet for Human Resources
P.O. Box 2150
Frankfort, KY 40601
(502) 564-2285

LOUISIANA
Support Enforcement Services
Department of Social Services
P.O. Box 94065
Baton Rouge, LA 70804-4065
(504) 342-4780

MAINE
Support Enforcement and Location
Bureau of Social Welfare
Department of Human Services
State House, Station 11
Augusta, ME 04333
(207) 289-2886

MARYLAND
Child Support Enforcement
Administration
Department of Human Resources
311 W. Saratoga, 3rd Floor
Baltimore, MD 31201
(410) 767-7674

MASSACHUSETTS
Child Support Enforcement Unit
Department of Revenue
141 Portland
Cambridge, MA 02139
(617) 577-7200

MICHIGAN
Office of Child Support
Department of Social Services
235 Grand Avenue
P.O. Box 30037
Lansing, MI 48909
(517) 373-7570

MINNESOTA
Office of Child Support
Department of Human Services
444 Lafayette, 4th Floor
St. Paul, MN 55155
(612) 651-2499

MISSISSIPPI
Child Support Division
State Department of Public Welfare
P.O. Box 352, 515 E. Amite Street
Jackson, MS 39205
(601) 354-0341, Ext. 503

MISSOURI
Child Support Enforcement Unit
Division of Legal Services
Dept. of Social Services
P.O. Box 1527 Jefferson City, MO
65102-1527
(573) 751-4301

MONTANA
Child Support Enforcement Program
Department of Social &
    Rehabilitative Services
P.O. Box 5955
Helena, MT 59604
(406) 444-4614

NEBRASKA
Child Support Enforcement Office
Department of Social Services
P.O. Box 95026
Lincoln, NE 68509
(402) 471-9125

NEVADA
Child Support Enforcement Program
Department of Human Resources
2527 N. Carson Street
Capital Complex
Carson City, NV 89710
(702) 885-4744

NEW HAMPSHIRE
Office of Child Support Enforcement
    Services
Division of Welfare
Health & Welfare Building
6 Hazen Drive
Concord, NH 03301
(603) 271-4426

NEW JERSEY
New Jersey Division of Public
    Welfare
Bureau of Child Support & Paternity
P.O. Box 715
Trenton, NJ 08625
(609) 588-2401

NEW MEXICO
Child Support Enforcement Bureau
Department of Human Services
P.O. Box 25109
Santa Fe, NM 87504
(505) 827-7200

NEW YORK
Office of Child Support
    Enforcement
New York State
Dept. of Social Services
P.O. Box 14
1 Commerce Plaza
Albany, NY 12260
(518) 474-9081

NORTH CAROLINA
Child Support Enforcement Section
Division of Social Services
Department of Human Resources
100 E. Six Forks
Raleigh, NC 27609
(919) 571-4120

NORTH DAKOTA
Child Support Enforcement
    Agency
North Dakota Dept. of Human
    Resources
State Capital
Bismark, ND 58505
(701) 224-3582

OHIO
Bureau of Child Support
Ohio Dept. of Human Services
State Office Tower
30 East Broad Street-27th Fl
Columbus, OH 43266-0423
(614) 466-3233

OKLAHOMA
Division of Child Support
Department of Human Services
P.O. Box 25352
Oklahoma City, OK 73125
(405) 424-5871

OREGON
Recovery Services Section
Adult and Family Services Div.
Department of Human Resources
P.O. Box 14506
Salem, OR 97309
(503) 378-5439

PENNSYLVANIA
Child Support Programs
Bureau of Claim Settlement
P.O. Box 8018
Harrisburg, PA 17105
(717) 783-8729

PUERTO RICO
Child Support Enforcement
Program
Department of Social Services
CALL Box 3349
San Juan, PR 00904
(809) 722-4731

RHODE ISLAND
Bureau of Family Support
Department of Social &
       Rehabilitative Services
77 Dorance
Providence, RI 02903
(401) 222-2409

SOUTH CAROLINA
Child Support Enforcement Division
Department of Social Services
P.O. Box 1520
Columbia, SC 29202-9988
(803) 737-9938

SOUTH DAKOTA
Office of Child Support Enforcement
Department of Social Services
700 Governors Drive
Pierre, SD 57501-2291
(605) 773-3641

TENNESSEE
Child Support Services
Department of Human Services
Citizens Plaza Bldg. 12th Floor
400 Deadrick Street
Nashville, TN 37248
(615) 313-4880

TEXAS
Child Support Enforcement Division
c/o Attorney General's Office
P.O. Box 12017
Austin, TX 78711-2017
(512) 231-4600

UTAH
Office of Recovery Services
Department of Social Services
120 N. 200 West
P.O. Box 45011
Salt Lake City, UT 84145-0011
(801) 538-4400

VERMONT
Child Support Division
Department of Social Welfare
103 South Main Street
Waterbury, VT 05671-1901
(802) 241-2319

VIRGINIA
Division of Support Enforcement
Department of Social Services
8007 Discovery Drive
Richmond, VA 23288
(804) 662-9629

WASHINGTON
Office of Support Enforcement
    Revenue Division
Department of Social & Health
    Services
Mailstop HJ-31
Olympia, WA 98504
(206) 459-6481

WEST VIRGINIA
Office of Child Support
    Enforcement
Department of Human Services
State Capital Complex
Building #6, Room 812
Charleston, WV 25305
(304) 348-3780

VIRGIN ISLANDS
Support and Paternity Division
Department of Justice
48B-50C Kronprindsens Gade
GERS Complex – 2nd Floor
St. Thomas, VI 00802
(809) 776-0372

WISCONSIN
Division of Community Services
Office of Child Support
201 E. Washington Avenue, Rm. 271
Madison, WI 53707-7935
(608) 266-9909

WYOMING
Child Support Enforcement Section
Division of Public Assistance &
    Social Services
State Dept. of Health & Social Services
Hathaway Building
Cheyenne, WY 82002
(307) 777-7892

GUAM
Office of the Attorney General
Union Bank
194 Hernan Cortez Avenue
Agana, Guam 96910
(671) 477-2036

Appendix C: Military Locator Service

UNITED STATES ARMY
Commander
United States Army
Finance and Accounting Center
Attn: FINCL
Indianapolis, IN 46249
(317) 510-2155

UNITED STATES AIR FORCE
Air Force Academy Finance Center
Attn: RPT
Denver, CO 80279-5000
(512) 652 5774

UNITED STATES NAVY
Navy Finance Center
Retired Pay Department Code 301
1240 East 9th Street
Cleveland OH 44199-2058
1-800-321-1080

UNITED STATES MARINES CORP
Marine Corps Finance Center
Code CPR
Kansas City, MO 64197-0001
(202) 694-1614

UNITED STATES COAST GUARD
Commanding Officer
U.S. Coast Guard Pay and Personnel Center
444 Southeast Quincy Street
Topeka, KS 66683
(785) 2952657

Appendix D: Frequently Asked Questions

Does child support have to be paid through the enforcement agency, or can my ex pay me directly?

Your ex can pay you directly if that is an arrangement that you both can live with. Before you make that decision, consider that if payments are made by wage withholding you will have a clear payment record through the CSE office, payments won't be delayed by the mail, and you avoid the possibility of money falling into the arrears by an ex who does not pay because *wage withholdings* are automatic. As long as the *obligor* keeps their job, you will receive child support. Having a wage withholding is beneficial for the *payor* as well due to some reports of *payee* not reporting the actual amount of support received.

Do I need a lawyer to petition for child support?

Having an attorney is not a requisite when petitioning for child support. If you can afford the benefit of hiring one - which may be costly - then it is always recommended that you do so. However, you may always represent yourself in court, or use one of many creative ways of hiring an attorney which may cost you nothing at all, or the bare minimum in up front fees. See chapters 5, 6, & 7

What is the difference between *alimony* and child support?

Alimony is a sum of money paid each month to a former spouse for their direct benefit. It could be used in a rehabilitative sense so that the receiver can go back to school to further enhance a career or change careers, or it can be used to keep the receiver up to the standard of living which they have been accustomed to, by being married to their former spouse. Child support is an amount of money paid to the custodial parent for the care of the children that were born to the payor and the payee.

Does it cost anything to apply for Child Support Enforcement Services?

Anyone who is receiving *AFDC*, Medicaid, or Foster Care stipends do not have to pay for CSE services. Everyone else can be charged a fee of up to $25.00.
Some states absorb all, or part, of the fee, and some states will collect the fee from the non-custodial parent. Check with your local CSE agency regarding your state policy.

Does it cost anything to receive services from CSE agencies?

CSE agencies can recover all, or part, of their fees from those who do not receive AFDC benefits. Fees can be deducted from child support payments, or collected from the *non-custodial* parent. Not all states recover the costs of their services so it's important to check with your local agencies regarding your state policies.

Do I need to know any of this since I have a lawyer?

Absolutely. We are always our own best advocates. By being well-informed and knowledgeable about child support guidelines and law, we can be certain that we ask the right questions and act on what is in our best interest.

If my child support is in the arrears can I withhold visitation?

No. Child support and *visitation* are separate issues. You cannot lawfully withhold visitation if child support is past due. Conversely, one cannot lawfully withhold child support if they are not allowed visitation. Many states are working on methods to assist with visitation issues.

What are the benefits of establishing paternity?

Once *paternity* has been established, your child gains most of the legal rights that a child born within a marriage has. This includes, but is not limited to, child support, rights to the fathers medical and life insurance benefits, inheritance, social security and veterans benefits. For more on paternity, see Chapter 2

What if the alleged father denies paternity and refuses to take a paternity test?

As of October 1989, anyone involved in a contested paternity case must submit to genetic testing. If the accused father is served and fails to respond to the complaint against him, a *default judgement* will be entered in court establishing paternity. At the same time, a court order for support may be issued.

Can I have an attorney and still receive CSE services?

Yes. Your attorney can work with the CSE agency on your behalf.

Will I receive child support collected if I am on AFDC?

If you are on AFDC and the state is able to collect your child support, you will receive up to $50.00 each month from the support collected in addition to your regular grant from AFDC. The balance of the child support paid will go towards reimbursing the government for the benefits made to your family.

My ex owes me a lot of child support, but continuously shows up with brand new cars. How could this be allowed to happen? Aren't creditors aware of child support arrearages?

Not unless someone tells them! A report of child support arrearages must be made to the credit bureaus or they will not be properly informed. The law allows for child support arrearages to be placed on credit reports so creditors can be aware of their customers' complete financial picture. Someone just has to make it happen. See Chapter 10 to learn how to do this.

My ex pays me directly, but always bounces the child support checks. By the time I get paid it is always another 30 days or so. What can I do?

The law allows for a wage withholding when child support payments are behind 30 days or more. Child support payments would then be taken directly from your ex's pay eliminating the need for him or her to pay you directly. Also, it is a crime to bounce checks. Think about taking criminal action by reporting the bad check to your local police department.

What if my ex's employer refuses to withhold wages for child support?

Your ex's employer does not have a choice. Federal law dictates that an employer must withhold wages if ordered by a court to do so.

My ex owed me several thousand dollars before I took my case to the CSE agency. Is there any way to recoup that past due money?

Since the money was owed before the CSE agency became involved in your case, they will have to verify that the money is owed to you. What documentation do you have to prove your case? Bring whatever letter of agreements that you have pertaining to this matter to your caseworker. You may have to appear in court to present your documentation before any collection can take place.

My ex is incarcerated. Is there any way for me to receive child support payments?

Child support obligations are not discontinued if the obligor is unable to make the payments. The unpaid support will accrue until it is properly paid, unless you agree to have payments deferred until the non-custodial parent is released and working. But why would you do that? If, while, in prison there are wages earned through a work release program, these earnings can be *garnished* for child support. If the non-custodial parent has *assets* or *real property,* you can receive an *execution* whereby the property is seized and sold, and whatever support is owed to you is then paid. This can be complicated, and cost you some money. Only you can decide if it is worth it. See chapter 10

My ex threatened to file for bankruptcy if I continued to pursue child support. How would this affect me?

It may affect you and it may not. If it does affect you, there are different degrees to which it can and will. See chapter 20

My CSE agency is not doing all that they can do to enforce my case. Can I take it to Federal Court?

Yes. If your CSE agency has not had any response to requests for enforcement in another jurisdiction, you can take your case to Federal Court. The decision has to be made by the Federal Regional Office of Child Support Enforcement at the request of your caseworker and the State Enforcement Office. If you are not satisfied with the services you are receiving by your local CSE agency, ask your State agency for help. For more on effective complaining to CSE agencies, see Chapter 21

Simone Spence is a nationally recognized leader in the field of Child Support Enforcement. The impact from her groundbreaking research has given her a national presence. She is a sought after speaker and lecturer and is a frequent guest of television and radio programs. Ms. Spence writes and lectures full time and lives in New Jersey.

If you have comments or would like information about upcoming events or seminars, please contact Simone Spence at the address below:

Simone Spence
P.O. Box 5
Cedar Grove, NJ 07009

Major cards and debit cards accepted, or charge to your phone bill!

For product information call
1-877-4DeadBeat

Or visit us on the World Wide Web at:
www.1-800-Deadbeat.com

If you would like to be placed on the waiting list for a personal phone consultation on How to Collect Your Child Support, with Simone Spence, please call the telephone number listed below. Or, e-mail her through the web site.

The following number is for appointments, only.

973-509-6975

Simone Spence is proud to offer seminars, training, and workshops free of charge to government officials, mental health professionals and Social Service agencies on a limited basis. Please contact her in writing on official letterhead.